VERY SHORT INTRODU[...]
and accessible way into a ne[...]
have been translated into m[...]

D0522384

The series began in 1995 [...]
every discipline. The VSI libra[...]
Short Introduction to everything from Psychology and Philosophy of
Science to American History and Relativity—and continues to grow in
every subject area.

Very Short Introductions available now:

Available soon:

For more information visit our website

www.oup.com/vsi/

Robert Jones

BRANDING

A Very Short Introduction

OXFORD
UNIVERSITY PRESS

OXFORD
UNIVERSITY PRESS

Great Clarendon Street, Oxford, OX2 6DP,
United Kingdom

Oxford University Press is a department of the University of Oxford.
It furthers the University's objective of excellence in research, scholarship,
and education by publishing worldwide. Oxford is a registered trade mark of
Oxford University Press in the UK and in certain other countries

First edition published in 2017

Impression: 3

Published in the United States of America by Oxford University Press
198 Madison Avenue, New York, NY 10016, United States of America

British Library Cataloguing in Publication Data
Data available

Library of Congress Control Number: 2016962481

ISBN 978-0-19-874991-2

Printed in Great Britain by
Ashford Colour Press Ltd, Gosport, Hampshire

For Brian Boylan, friend and mentor

For Brian Paulin, friend and mentor

Contents

Contents

Thank you

I'd like to thank Mary Jo Hatch, who got this book off the ground by introducing me to its excellent editor, Andrea Keegan. Ije Nwokorie and Sairah Ashman at Wolff Olins have given me the time and space to write this book. Many people have helped along the way, including Val Allam, Hans Arnold, Deborah Cadbury, Hope Cooke, Anthony Galvin, Dan Gavshon-Brady, Tilde Heding, Kenny Jacobs, Nathan Jarvis, Peter McKenna, Chris Mitchell, Chris Moody, Jenny Nugée, and Jane Scruton. Craig Mawdsley gave me some particularly thoughtful feedback. My clients have expanded my ideas and horizons: Luqman Arnold, Dawn Austwick, Sally Cowdry, Michael Day, Stephen Deuchar, Cathy Ferrier, Danny Homan, Antony Jenkins, Stuart Lipton, Michelle McEttrick, Steve Morriss, Simon Nelson, Stephen Page, Farah Ramzan Golant, Fiona Reynolds, Chris Saul, Magnus Scheving, Nick Serota, David Souden, and James Tipple. My colleagues at the University of East Anglia have opened my eyes to many new angles on branding: in particular, I'd like to thank James Cornford, Paul Dobson, Nichola Johnson, Rose Kemmy, Ken Le Meunier-FitzHugh, Peter Schmidt-Hansen, and Nikos Tzokas. My students have constantly made me think. Brian Boylan has been my mentor for twenty years, and gave me his usual pin-sharp feedback. And my partner Neil McKenna has been generous as always, with warm encouragement and wise advice.

List of illustrations

Introduction

Every day, we're exposed to thousands of brand messages, whether we like it or not. The rise of brands has been phenomenal and unstoppable. Today, branding shapes and defines our world at every level, from the trivial to the profound.

Branding has been claimed as a science, as an art, and even as a dark corporate conspiracy. It's been studied by economists, marketers, designers, organizational specialists, psychologists, philosophers, social theorists, and cultural critics. Yet very few of these experts agree on what branding is, and how it works. It's important and exciting, but also amorphous, elusive, and ill-defined.

So this book aims to give you a quick guided tour. It suggests some straightforward answers to the big questions. What exactly is a brand? How did branding grow and spread? How do brands work on us? Who are the people behind the brands, and what do they do? Does branding guide us or enslave us? And where will branding go next?

Branding, as I hope to show, is more than it might appear. It's more than just an aspect of marketing: it's a broader activity, affecting most of the things an organization does. Following from that, its impact is not just on consumers: it's just as important as a force that guides and energizes employees. And, finally, branding has more than just a commercial impact. It's also a powerful social, cultural, and—in the widest sense—political force.

This Introduction is based not on textbooks, but on my twenty-five years' experience as a brand consultant. It's not the final word on branding—there never will be a final word—but I hope it will open your eyes to the extraordinary phenomenon of branding, and reveal a little about the work that goes on behind the scenes to shape the brands that surround us.

Chapter 1
The triumph of branding

In Malindi, Kenya, you'll find a poster painted on a bright red fence, showing a silhouette of a Coca-Cola bottle, and the slogan 'A billion reasons to believe in Africa'.

What it says is not that Coca-Cola will quench your thirst, but that Coca-Cola is somehow part of the optimism and growth of Africa. It suggests there are 'A billion reasons to believe in Africa'—which is presumably the billion people who live on that continent.

This African poster (see Figure 1) makes a fascinating snapshot of the strange phenomenon called branding. It shows, of course, that branding is everywhere, on every continent, urban and rural, rich and poor. And it shows how, in our globalized world, branding often tries to belong to a particular place too: this poster is aiming to make Coca-Cola feel distinctively African.

It shows that branding depends on signs—images that embody meaning. Brands are meanings ('signified'), recognizable through symbols such as logos ('signifiers'). And though it's part of a campaign launched back in 2012, the poster is painted, permanently, on a corrugated metal fence. Branding is not always ephemeral.

Though branding set out initially to sell consumer products, it often does more than that. It connects products with bigger ideas:

1. Branding at work: a poster in Malindi, Kenya, that suggests that Coca-Cola is not just a drink, but also a part of Africa's future.

sugary drinks, in this case, are connected with human progress. When you stop and think about it, this is a thought process that's bizarre, and almost magical. Coca-Cola's Global Brand Director Lorna Sommerville explains: 'When an idea taps into a fundamental human truth, there are no borders or boundaries to how far it can go'. Sometimes branding taps into 'truths': more often, perhaps, into universal hopes and aspirations.

So a brand is much more than just the name of a product. Around the world, mundane commercial products are plugging into bigger ideas, to make people feel good about the products, and to buy more of them. Every piece of branding hopes to get you to believe something. Branding aims to give us all 'billions of reasons to believe'.

Brands have been around for centuries, but the idea has become central to our lives since the 1980s. In the last thirty years or so, branding has become pervasive, reaching into even the poorest parts of the planet. In fact, it has become a defining characteristic of the modern world. How and why has this happened?

A larger idea

Branding connects ordinary things with a larger idea. This larger idea has the power to change what people do: in particular, to buy more and pay more. Coca-Cola is just flavoured, sugared water. It's the brand that makes it possible to charge good money for it, and that therefore makes money for the company. Disney's larger idea is 'family fun'; Volvo's is 'safety'. That is the essence of branding.

It's a technique used by the owners—the Coca-Cola Company, for example—to create meanings that make us feel good about the product, so that we'll buy it. Coca-Cola invests in communication that connects its product with ideas of progress, optimism, and happiness. When this communication works, these meanings form the Coca-Cola brand. And in the end people buy more Coca-Cola. Branding changes how people think, feel—and act.

But it's also a method used by consumers to help make sense of the plethora of products in the world. Surrounded by thousands of choices, people assign them meanings, so that they can mentally file them and strengthen their sense of their own identity. We might, for instance, associate Coca-Cola with energy, perhaps with memories of childhood, and many of us define ourselves as Coca-Cola people, as opposed to (for instance) Pepsi people. Branding is a game kicked off by the big corporations—but it's a game where almost everyone joins in. The ideal, for the corporation, is when the ideas in our minds match the ones they try to project.

The Coca-Cola poster is one example of a phenomenon that, in the last couple of decades, has become pervasive. Branding started with products like Coca-Cola. Then it moved into services—for example, banks like Wells Fargo, or retailers like Carrefour, or airlines like Emirates. Next, it reached corporations, like Cisco or Unilever or LG Group. More recently, branding has expanded its reach into books, films, and television series. *Harry Potter*, Beyoncé, *Star Wars*, and *Game of Thrones* all are more than books, singers, films, or shows: they're big global brands. Whole genres can become a brand, like Bollywood. And over the last twenty years, a batch of huge online brands has come to dominate the world, from Alibaba and Amazon to Instagram and Uber.

Though branding started in the West, it has spread across the world. Global brands, as we've seen, try to establish a local resonance. Home-grown brands mimic the attributes of the global mega-brands, with shiny logos, catchy slogans, and glossy packaging.

Branding has spread into small businesses too. There's a small chain of teashops in the north of England, called Bettys, that's a model of branding: it uses its Swiss/Yorkshire heritage to add ideas of precision, daintiness, and warmth to the ordinary business of food and drink. As city districts get gentrified, even small shops get sophisticated design work done, and aspire to become brands. Every online start-up has an element of branding behind it. And everywhere we go, we see branding in action. I'm writing this in the British Library, in a space called not 'The Newspaper Archive' but, more excitingly, 'Newsroom'. This too is branding.

The greatest commercial invention?

Branding is, of course, good at getting people to buy things. Brands play a role in many of our day-to-day buying decisions—both big decisions, like choosing an Apple tablet, or small ones, like believing my cat prefers a brand of cat litter called Thomas. Brands add excitement to, and reduce the anxiety in, shopping.

There are limits, though, to the power of branding. Many products actually have very little additional meaning. When we buy a pencil, or fill up with petrol, or take out an insurance policy, the brand we choose may well have no deep associations in our minds. One study showed that, though 80 per cent of marketing directors believe their products are 'differentiated', or have some distinctive meaning in consumers' minds, only 10 per cent of consumers would agree. For most products, most of the time, most people simply don't have time to care. Each of us has the mental space for only a few brands. For me, these might be Apple, the BBC, and the retailer Waitrose, but very few more. Underlining that, a study by the media agency Havas Media suggests that most people wouldn't care if 74 per cent of brands disappeared. People buy brands, and they buy into branding, but they like to be sceptical too. We find fanciful television advertising absurd: in fact, we probably fast-forward through it. We pride ourselves on seeing through companies' branding activities.

And yet brands are the primary source of value for many companies. When you look at the value of a typical business, you find that some of it comes from its buildings, equipment, and stock—its tangible assets—but a lot too from intangible assets, like customer goodwill, or patents, or its brand. In fact, the global market research consultancy Millward Brown reckons that brand accounts for more than 30 per cent of the stockmarket value of America's biggest companies, and we'll see why in Chapter 4. For some kinds of company, brand is less important: it matters relatively little to, say, an office cleaning business. But for others, such as luxury goods companies, it's worth up to 90 per cent of their value. Overall, around a third of all the corporate value in the world comes from branding. By any standards, this makes branding one of the most effective commercial inventions of all time.

The most potent cultural form?

As we've seen, most people are aware of the phenomenon of branding. They discuss it, interpret it, and critique it. As well as an effective commercial technique, branding is also part of our shared culture.

Brands are a social reference point, something we all have in common. When my students meet each other for the first time each September, they bond within hours, at least in part because they have brands in common—whether it's Evian or Beats or Louis Vuitton, it's recognizable and means roughly the same thing everywhere, and people define themselves (and others) by the brands they like. There's even a board game, the Logo Game, where players compete on their knowledge of branding.

Brands are also one of the devices we use to remember the past. This comes across particularly strongly at the Museum of Brands in London, where visitors walk through a time tunnel of packaging and advertising, from about 1890 onwards. As they get closer to the present day, the overwhelming response is of nostalgia: the most common reaction among visitors is 'ah, I remember that'. Brands give an instant short-cut. For me, the

Thunderbirds brand takes me to the 1960s, Doc Martens to the 1970s, Audi to the 1980s, and so on.

Brand thinking pervades so much of our life. Brands have helped us sensitize ourselves to the interplay of signifier and signified. Signifiers—what things are called, and what they look like—really matter. Political correctness is an example of branding: carefully re-labelling things in order to shift how people think and feel about them. In one way, the liberal consensus is that labels shouldn't matter; in another way, they inevitably do.

Brands are frequently used or exploited by artists and writers. Indeed, there's an affinity between branding and art, as two parallel methods for making meaning. Edouard Manet's last major work was 'A Bar at the Folies-Bergère', an 1882 painting of a disaffected barmaid, one of those whom Guy de Maupassant described as 'vendors of drink and of love'. At the bottom right of the painting is a bottle of Bass beer, whose logo was the very first trademark to be legally registered, only five years before in 1877. Manet made an image that's interpreted by an audience to create meaning—and he included the Bass logo, which does exactly the same thing.

Many see brands as a negative force in culture. There's a Canadian group of anti-consumerists called Adbusters who describe themselves as 'artists, activists, writers, pranksters, students, educators and entrepreneurs'. Adbusters create powerful parodies of brand advertising, which they call 'subvertisements'. They use the techniques of branding to attack branding, and Adbusters has become a brand in its own right.

Perhaps the most powerful critics have been artists themselves. Brands are a quick way to signal people's status or aspirations, and an easy way to satirize a materialist society—a technique pioneered by Cyra McFadden in *The Serial* in 1977, and adopted by Bret Easton Ellis eight years later in *Less Than Zero*. More recently, artists such as the Chapman brothers have used brand imagery in a more savage critique of consumer culture, and the Chinese artist Ai Weiwei has painted the Coca-Cola logo onto ancient vases: a gesture that both vandalizes the vase and yet somehow beautifies the logo.

But at the same time, other artists have played along with branding, and see no conflict between commercialism and higher culture. Films lovingly embrace brands as a quick way to communicate information about characters and situations, from James Bond's Aston Martin onwards. And is it an accident that the heroine of the 2014 science fiction film *Interstellar* is called 'Brand', and the implication of the film's ending is that she is the future? Most famously, perhaps, Andy Warhol adopted the imagery of branding in works like his 1972 piece 'Campbell's Soup Cans'. Warhol was criticized for capitulating to consumerism, but wrote 'Making money is art, and working is art, and good business is the best art'.

The last thirty years

Branding, then, is a pervasive system of signs, associated with products, services, organizations, cultural products, places, people, even concepts. These signs help give those things additional meanings not inherent in them. It's been around for centuries, as we'll see in Chapter 3, but it's become a central part of culture relatively recently.

Google's 'ngram viewer' is a clever bit of software that counts the occurrences of a given word in all the books that Google has digitized, and shows how the number of occurrences changes over time. The graph for the word 'brand' is flat until 1900, grows slowly until 1940, plateaus, then climbs again from 1980 onwards, accelerating rapidly at the end of the millennium. The academic study of branding, focusing on the concept of 'brand equity', also took off in the 1980s. Why has branding become such a pervasive concept, particularly in the last thirty years?

The triumph of market economics has created a world of global competition, where organizations must use branding to stand out from their rivals. Everywhere is now a market—including, in the last thirty years, China. And these local markets all merge into a global one. Shareholders demand that publicly quoted organizations constantly grow, which means increasing market share, or opening up new markets. Governments need state-owned organizations to hold their own, sometimes competing with foreign rivals in the home or export markets—so they too must play the brand game. Even monopolies are competing for something—to attract funding at the right price, or to attract the best possible employees.

And it's not just companies that are competing. Countries and cities compete to attract tourists, employers, students, and residents. Not-for-profit, sports clubs, political parties, and even religions compete to attract supporters. Branding is currently a hot topic in the world's two biggest industries, healthcare and education: hospitals, universities, and schools are taking their brands very seriously. In all these areas, in the last decade or so, it has become acceptable, and even fashionable, to use the language and techniques of branding. Ten years ago, people in museums, for example, rejected the notion of branding as commercial and reductive. But now, almost all museums readily talk about the importance of their brands. Because the internet is a global medium, all are competing across borders, which means that the same kinds of concepts and techniques rapidly expand everywhere.

This rise in the power of the market, this rise in materialism, has given people an increasing need for meaning in their lives, both as consumers and as employees. Human beings have always needed meaning, a dimension beyond the utilitarian, beyond the mundane things we all have to do from day to day. People need a sense of identity (who am I?) and belonging (where do I fit?). In the past, these meanings came from family, village, religion, nation—but all have been undermined by urbanization, secularization, and globalization. Materialism creates a vacuum of meaning—and then branding tries to fill that vacuum. Consumers need not just 'value for money' but *values* for money'.

In response, a particular kind of branding has become mainstream—seeing brand as not a product but a concept. That Coca-Cola poster in Kenya (Figure 1) is a perfect example. Many companies have become excited by the idea that they can be more than just manufacturers of material products: they can also be purveyors of ideas or even *ideals* that enrich culture and give people new senses of identity. Apple, Virgin, and IKEA are clear examples—all businesses that were either born in, or took off in, the last thirty years.

Identity and belonging

And, over the same period, consumers have joined in this game. Branding has shifted from something that companies do to us, into a game that most of us join in. Academics, over the same timescale, have shifted from a positivist to a constructivist view of branding—in other words, they see brands as things we all help to construct.

As people have become richer, with more access to more goods, they've started to define themselves partly through seemingly mundane choices: the shoes they wear, the shop where they bought their furniture, the box sets they watch, the companies they admire, or even their favourite sugary drink. They use brands to help construct their identity, their sense of who they are. For good or ill, millions, perhaps even billions, of people—from an African village to a Shanghai penthouse to a mid-west mall—use brands to help form their self-image, or to help define the 'tribe' they want to belong to.

Of course, brands aren't the only option. Clearly, many identify themselves with the charities they support, the sports clubs they follow, the political parties they vote for, the places they visit, or the celebrities they admire. Many people resist branding, and a few are immune. Brands, for them, have none of this glamorous power. And—after a decade of company scandals and financial crashes—there's an increasingly anti-corporate spirit in the world.

Yet for many, particularly younger people, branding has become so pervasive, so *normal*, that it's lost its sting. They find it natural to play the branding game, and also to see branding as more than just a commercial phenomenon. They pick and mix ideas from a whole range of brands—not just Adidas and Apple but also Vimeo and Vice—and use them as components to create senses of identity. They do this through social media, so it's a shared activity, and one where fashions constantly move on, so that their identities morph.

By taking part in the magical activity of branding, people add value to the things around them, they become more than themselves, they acquire meaning—not least because everyone around them is doing it too. Often that meaning sits between me and you. I'm a customer of a British bank called First Direct, and if I see another customer with a First Direct card ahead of me in the checkout queue, I feel an odd sense of affinity. I feel that because we've both chosen the same bank, he or she must be a bit like me.

And in the age of social media, where it's instinctive to share things minute by minute, it's no surprise that brands—an easy token for sharing meaning—have become so central to our lives and our imaginations. Sharing of 'content' has become an almost universal habit. It's now normal to post on Facebook the moment something has happened, or even while it's happening. In this new culture of sharing, it's easy for brands to thrive and grow. And the phenomenon goes further: every time someone posts something on Facebook or Twitter or Instagram, they are nurturing ideas about who they are. Deliberately or not, they are building their own personal brand. In this sense, the world now contains almost two billion brand marketers.

Both commerce and culture

The modern world is defined by a whole range of phenomena, from social media to climate change, from urbanization to obesity, from mass migration to the cult of celebrity. But one of them—so pervasive that we take it for granted—is branding.

Because the logic of the market is now so ubiquitous, and the need for a shared sense of identity has become so urgent, branding has become a defining characteristic of the modern world.

Through branding, boring things like detergents, everyday things like soft drinks, and intangible things like websites have acquired personalities and meanings, so that people recommend them, feel partisanship, forgive them their failings—all because organizations need to compete, and people need to feel and share meanings.

Branding is now one of the most potent forces, commercial and cultural, on the planet. But what exactly is it? (Box 1)

Box 1 Android: no-one's and everyone's

Android could be the biggest brand on earth, with a billion users and a 90 per cent market share. But it's not a company: it's a brand that's shared by 400 companies. And that's the secret of its success. Google released Android in 2008, as an operating system for mobile devices that would be customizable, accessible, and above all open, and now it's used in phones, tablets, watches, cars, and more. Legally, the brand belongs to Google, and manufacturers buy a licence. But emotionally, the brand belongs to everyone and no-one. And rather than enforcing consistency among all the manufacturers that use it, it encourages variation. Its slogan 'Be together, not the same' captures a lot about current trends in branding.

Chapter 2
What is 'branding'?

To define 'branding', we need to start by defining 'brand'. When we talk about 'the Netflix brand' or 'the H&M brand' or 'the Alibaba brand', what do we really mean?

Perhaps a brand is simply a name: 'Netflix' or 'H&M' or 'Alibaba'. But not every trade name is a brand. Think about your local back-street car repair business, for instance. It has a name—'Webster's Autos', or something like that—and locally it might be well-respected. It might have 'a good name', as people say. But we wouldn't naturally call it a brand. We tend to think a brand is deliberately designed in a more sophisticated way than the work of the local sign-painter.

So is it the design that makes the difference? Is a brand a logo, or a particular colour, or perhaps a slogan? The swoosh of Nike, the red of Manchester United, the 'Power of dreams' slogan of Honda? This is how Wikipedia defines 'brand': 'a name, term, design, symbol or other feature that distinguishes one seller's product from those of others'. But this definition doesn't account for the power of brands—if they were just decorative items that we see around us, they'd be much less interesting.

So maybe a brand is more about the product itself? Indeed, it's often very hard to separate 'brand' and 'product' in our minds.

What is it that people love, the Apple product or the Apple brand—or are they the same thing? The Al Jazeera news service is very close to the Al Jazeera brand. But they're not identical. It's possible to like the brand but not the product, or vice versa. My favourite car brand is Audi, but I actually decided to buy a BMW.

Bigger than a product

Indeed, a brand is somehow bigger than a product. We sometimes see it as the aura around a product, or the ethos beneath a product, or the provenance behind a product. People sometimes use the word 'make' to mean 'brand'—'Aga is a good make of cooker'—meaning not just that it's a good cooker, but also that the company that made it is widely admired. Fans of Apple tell you that they admire the products, but they also admire the vision behind the products—and some worry that, after the death of Steve Jobs, the vision will slowly fade. A contestant on the British version of the reality television show *The Apprentice* called himself 'Stuart Baggs the brand', meaning that he was more than just a person, he was somehow a bigger set of ideas. And clearly, that's what Coca-Cola is trying to do with its poster in Kenya (Figure 1).

So a brand is something extra to a product. The branding expert Martin Kornberger has said that a brand is 'functionality + meaning': that is, the product plus an idea. In his view, the brand is the whole thing—the Toblerone brand is the chocolate bar, plus meanings to do with Switzerland, the Alps, and so on.

Conversely, the marketer Phil Barden suggests that 'brands are frames: they implicitly influence the perceived value of products and product experiences through framing'. On this view, the product is like a picture, and the brand is an additional frame round that picture, giving it context and potency. The chocolate bar is the picture, and the Swissness is a frame that makes the chocolate bar more interesting, memorable, and valuable.

This additional meaning is key to the power of brands. Brands get us to do things, they change behaviour, they create value, and that's because they're not static images on paper, they're dynamic ideas in our minds. A simple way to put this is: a product's brand is what it *stands for*. Webster's Autos doesn't stand for anything, beyond just being a car repair place, so it's not a brand. The Nike swoosh is not what Nike stands for, so it's not a brand either—it's just a signifier of that larger meaning, about challenge and achievement. And Corona is a great product, but its brand stands for something more than the beer, to do with Mexico, the summer, and the beach. The product on its own is not a brand.

Standing for something

Importantly, 'standing for something' can mean two different things, depending on your perspective.

Looking from inside the organization, it can mean your internal ethos, your identity: the ideas you *want* to stand for. IKEA wants to stand for the idea of 'creating a better everyday life for the many people'. That's its official vision statement, in its wilfully odd English (Figure 2). Most organizations elaborately define their brand, and actively manage it, as we'll see in Chapter 5.

But looking from outside, it can mean your associations, your meanings, your image: the ideas you *actually* stand for in people's minds. If you ask people what's in their heads when they think about IKEA, they will say obvious things like 'furniture', 'kitchens', 'flat pack', and 'store', but also aspects of the shopping experience like 'meatballs', 'day trip', or 'queue', and bigger thoughts like 'design', 'life', or even 'love'. This is the exciting reality of a brand: a cluster of potent ideas in people's minds that influence where they choose to go, and what they choose to buy.

These are two very different angles on 'brand'.

2. Shopping at IKEA: an experience from which customers form their impression of the IKEA brand, including quality and price, but also design and lifestyle.

Practitioners—the people who manage brands and the people who advise them—naturally tend to have an insider view. Some managers take their brand very seriously. General Electric wants to stand for the idea of 'imagination at work', and its CEO, Jeff Immelt, has said: 'For GE, imagination at work is more than a slogan or a tagline. It is a reason for being.' Advertising agencies often see a brand as the big idea that is the fount of all their communication work. The advertising guru David Ogilvy said: 'Unless your advertising contains a big idea, it will pass like a ship in the night'. Specialist branding consultancies see a brand as a set of ideas that should influence not only communication, but everything an organization does. Brand expert Rita Clifton champions it as 'the central organizing principle in successful businesses'. On this view, a brand is a set of ideas inside an organization.

Academics, though, looking analytically at brands as a phenomenon, tend to take the outsider view. Business school academics often see a brand as a group of associations in consumers' minds that influence buying behaviour. Of course, there are many variations on this: indeed, there are probably as many theories as there are academics. Across the campus, another breed of academics specializing in cultural studies tend to focus on brands as signs, performing a central role in consumer culture—but again they take an outsider view, and often a highly critical one.

Martin Kornberger's book *Brand Society* neatly links the two views, seeing brands as things that transform both management (the insider view) and lifestyle (the outsider view)—things that link production (insider) with consumption (outsider).

Defining 'brand'

So a brand is what you stand for internally, and what you stand for externally. The branding academic David Aaker refers to the internal version as 'identity' and the external version as 'image'. 'Brand' means both identity and image. But which view should we take as the primary definition? Which view best captures the power of a brand? Which is the 'real' brand: the identity the company intended, or the image the rest of us see? Whose view is clearer: the practitioner's or the academic's?

Though my background is as a practitioner, I'm struck by the words of the branding academic Kevin Lane Keller: 'The power of a brand lies in what resides in the minds of customers'. So for this book, we're adopting the external view: a brand is primarily the 'ideas and feelings a commercial, organizational or cultural entity stands for in people's minds'.

The Whole Foods Market brand is a cluster of associations in people's minds about quality, healthiness, organics, and premium prices. The Ryanair brand brings ideas in people's minds about low prices, a no-nonsense attitude, and basic levels of service. The Samsung brand is ideas about clever new technology, shiny design, and mid-level pricing. And so on.

Amazon's Jeff Bezos seems to reinforce this view when he describes a brand as 'what people say about you when you're not in the room'. It's a neat definition—and a scary one for practitioners. But it may be that his formula is a definition of 'reputation' rather than 'brand'. The two concepts are very close to each other, but reputation tends to be more a rational, verbal thing, an account of what you've done, when brand is often more emotional, more visual, and a belief about what I'll get from you in the future. It's possible, indeed, for a company to have a bad reputation and a good brand at the same time. Consumers say bad things about it, but keep buying from it. Ironically, Amazon is itself a great example of this phenomenon.

Brand expert Marty Neumeier captures the more emotional side. He defines brand as 'a person's gut feeling about a product, service or organisation'. This raises the question of which person he has in mind, and maybe therefore it's best to conceive of a brand as the combination of everyone's gut feelings. Or, to be more complete, because brands aren't only emotional, the sum total of everyone's thoughts and feelings: in a word, their ideas.

Not just ideas

But a brand is not just ideas. Brands are founded on material things. The Whole Foods Market, Ryanair, and Samsung brands don't come from nowhere: they're shaped by what those organizations say and do. Our ideas about Nescafé are partly shaped by decades of advertising—by what Nescafé says. Our ideas about Spotify depend on the quality, day by day, of the user experience—by what Spotify does. Coca-Cola isn't just an abstract idea about progress in Africa—it's also a sweet, fizzy drink. Behind the ideas there's the substance.

And the fascinating thing about brands is that they all seem to have a symbol, badge, or label—a distinctive style. Going back to

Wikipedia's definition, brands do have interesting names, terms, designs, symbols, and other features. Every brand has a brand name, and almost every brand has a logo. BP has its green and yellow colours; Burberry, its check pattern; Michelin, its tyre-man; London Underground, its typeface. Nike has its slogan, 'just do it', and *The Economist* has a distinctive writing style. Singapore Airlines even has its own smell. Confusingly, this is often referred to as 'brand identity': in branding, 'identity' can mean both 'what we want to stand for' and 'the symbols we use'. These symbols often appeal directly to the more intuitive or more emotional parts of our minds—to what Neumeier calls our 'gut feeling'.

So for the purposes of this book, a brand is:

- a set of *ideas* and feelings about a product or other entity
- shaped by what that product *says and does*
- and recognized through a distinctive *style*.

For example, the McDonald's brand is a set of ideas about burgers, children, comfort food, 'happy meals', and many other things. It's shaped by our experience over many years of its restaurants and of its advertising. And it's symbolized by devices like the golden arches and the Ronald McDonald character.

The MINI brand, to take another example, is a set of ideas about individuality, clever design, urban driving, and adventure. It's shaped by years of advertising, as well as by the very distinctive small cars with a wheel at each corner—and also by films featuring the cars, like *The Italian Job*. And it's symbolized by the MINI logo and the particular shape of the MINI radiator grille.

This, then, is our working definition—one that starts to explain the power of brands in our minds, and how those ideas lodge themselves in our minds. But however we choose to define 'brand', people actually use the word much more loosely.

Very often, it's used to mean 'a branded product or company'—for example, 'the British Airways brand is struggling against its lower-cost rivals'. Sometimes, it's used to mean just the logo: marketing directors often ask their advertising agencies to 'make our brand bigger on this advert'. And sometimes 'brand' is used to mean the activity of branding. Marketing people say things like 'the goal of the Hyundai brand is to increase market share'.

The truth is that the word is a complex one, useful because its meaning is so fuzzy. The concept, in fact, bridges all sorts of gaps. A brand sits at the interface between the concrete and the abstract: between a product and an idea. It links the internal and the external: the 'identity' a company wants to stand for and the 'image' it actually stands for. It bridges the employee's world of production and the customer's world of consumption. It combines form and function: the logo and the product. And it embraces both commerce and culture.

Brand and branding

What's the difference between 'brand' and 'branding'? Branding, simply, is the set of things a brand owner does to establish a brand. If a brand is 'what you stand for', branding is a technique through which a company gets its product to stand for something in the minds of millions. 'Branding' is the activity, 'brand' the result: 'branding' is the cause, 'brand' is the effect.

When people talk about branding (or 'rebranding') something, they normally mean trying to impress a new set of ideas into people's minds about it. They might also mean giving it a new style (name, logo, colours, or whatever), as a way of accelerating that change of mind. When the British retailer the Co-op rebranded, it wanted to change how people think and feel about the business—and it signalled that change through a new logo.

In doing this kind of thing, brand managers are trying to close the gap between 'image' and 'identity': to get what their product actually stands for as close as possible to what they want it to stand for. For strong brands like Apple, the gap is small; for weaker brands, it's much wider. Sometimes this means returning to the past: the Co-op chose not to design a new logo but to return to a previous one, aiming to rekindle in consumers' minds old ideas about local convenience, ethical trading, and value-for-money.

All of this, of course, is done to improve the business's commercial performance. Branding aims to get people not just to change their ideas but also to change their behaviour—most obviously, to buy more—and we'll explore this in much more detail in Chapter 4. The branding efforts of eBay are designed to get more and more people to go to eBay for new products—to see it as a retailer, not just an auction site. For not-for-profit organizations, branding might aim for social rather than commercial goals. Change.org, for example, uses its branding to encourage people to join campaigns that change government policy. And more and more commercial organizations aim for social goals too—Unilever is a prime example. Indeed they see social and commercial impact as a virtuous circle—the better citizen you are, the happier consumers will be to buy from you.

So we can start to define branding: shaping what the product or organization says and does, in order to change how people think, feel, and act, in a way that creates commercial (and sometimes also social) value.

Same and different

Branding, then, starts by changing how people think and feel: it's about creating, or changing, meanings. And this is a delicate task.

To create meaning, you have to start by conforming to convention—to be similar to others—or people won't understand you at all.

Language and symbols work through conventional meanings. An airline needs to look a bit like other airlines. Fashion retailers like New Look, Primark, and Top Shop have surprisingly similar logos. When setting out to brand anything—from a fruit juice to a university—you have to conform to some extent to the conventions of fruit juices or universities, in what you do, what you say, and how you look. Otherwise people won't understand what you are, and they won't trust you.

But you have to be different too, and maybe even break conventions, or you'll fail to say anything new and people won't notice you. And branding tends to push towards difference, towards standing out from the crowd, away from conformity. 'Branding is all about creating differences', as Kevin Lane Keller says. The more different, the greater the risk, but also potentially the higher the reward. When Tate's new branding designs were presented to trustees in 1999, they were resisted: 'That's not what a proper art gallery looks like'. But the designs did get used, got noticed, helped Tate double its visitor numbers, and now seem normal, a new convention. Some branding experts aim for what they call 'MAYA', meaning 'most advanced yet acceptable'.

So brands are in some ways the same as their rivals, and in other ways different. They're also fundamentally the same from one country to another. Consistency matters: otherwise, whenever we travel, our expectations would be confounded and our trust would be broken. But even chains like Starbucks or McDonald's, which appear to be almost identical everywhere, in practice differ to suit local tastes. Hotel chains aim for a reassuring global consistency, but most also encourage local variation. Part of a good global brand's meaning is about familiarity and predictability and reassurance, but part too is about variation and surprise and local colour.

As well as being similar from one place to another, brands mostly stay the same from one year to the next. We rely on continuity:

most brands get their power from familiarity, going back into childhood, like Disney, Heinz, Mars, or Johnson & Johnson. But equally, no brand can stand still. Consumers change, attitudes change, technologies change, and branding must subtly morph too. The speed of change varies: a fashion brand may shift quickly, an infrastructure brand much more slowly. But all branding creates meaning that's partly about permanence and heritage and maturity, partly about dynamism and the future and youthfulness.

The task of branding, then, is a lot to do with deciding just how much to be the same as your competitors, and the same from one country to another, and the same as you were last year—and just how much to be different.

Making meaning, making value

So branding helps a product or organization to stand for something, and therefore to stand out. For example, IKEA creates advertising carefully designed to suggest a particular lifestyle. It designs products and stores that make design affordable to everyone. It carefully manages its symbols, such as its blue and yellow colours, its logo, and its quirky product names. And all of this helps it to stand for 'a better everyday life for the many people'. This is the height of contemporary global branding.

Branding does all of this for a reason: to change how we act, in ways that create value. Branding creates brands—meanings, ideas in our minds—in order to influence what we do. It gets consumers to buy, and employees to work hard, in order to achieve the commercial goals of profit and growth—and also sometimes social goals like wellbeing and sustainability. IKEA's branding attracts customers, encourages them to visit often and buy more, and supports the growth of IKEA into more and more countries round the world. But it also nudges consumers into greener ways of living, by making low-energy light-bulbs the norm, and by moving towards what it calls the 'circular economy', where customers can not only buy new furniture but also sell back old items for others to re-use.

So branding changes minds in order to create many different kinds of value (Box 2). But its contemporary scope and power, illustrated by the IKEA example, is a recent thing. Over the centuries, branding has changed, grown, and expanded dramatically.

Box 2 Etsy: a platform for makers

Etsy is a platform that helps craftspeople sell their products worldwide—and so to build brands themselves. It was founded in 2005 by Robert Kalin in Brooklyn, NY, as 'an online community where crafters, artists and makers could sell their handmade and vintage goods and craft supplies'. More grandly, Etsy says its mission is 'to reimagine commerce in ways that build a more fulfilling and lasting world'. Etsy now connects 1.6 million active sellers with 26 million active buyers, selling $2.4 billion worth of stuff every year. Like eBay, it's a great example of a platform brand, giving sellers a marketplace on a scale never before possible. Unlike eBay, it plays to another great trend of our times: the desire not just to consume things but also to make them.

Chapter 3
The history of branding

It's 1865, and George Cadbury is in the Netherlands inspecting
a new machine that makes cocoa. His family has sold tea, coffee,
and drinking chocolate in Birmingham since 1824. He's a Quaker by
religion, an idealist who wants to give people healthy, non-alcoholic
drinks. He's also a businessman who needs to make money, because
Quakers who go bankrupt have to leave the sect. Later, at the end
of the century, he'll introduce progressive innovations for his
workers too—airy factories, holidays, schools, even a whole village,
called Bournville.

But back in 1865, he's fascinated by this new Dutch machine,
because it solves the great cocoa problem. Cocoa is naturally full
of fats, which make for an unpleasant drink. Traditionally, those
fats are stripped out using additives, including harmful things
like sawdust. But this machine hydraulically presses the cocoa
beans, and squashes out much of the fat. For the first time,
Cadbury can offer the people of Britain a chocolate drink that
really is pure (Figure 3).

And over the succeeding years, Cadbury made not just a product,
but also a brand. As early as 1867, he started advertising (which
didn't come naturally to plain-living Quakers). He used a bold
slogan: 'Absolutely Pure, Therefore Best'. He launched the slogan
in an unmissable campaign on London's horse-drawn buses.

3. A brand pioneer: a Cadbury poster from 1888 that sells cocoa through the imagery of purity.

Cadbury promoted not just cocoa but the idea of *purity*. He commissioned advertising that showed children, the symbols of purity. He even launched a campaign for purity in food products. Decades ahead of his time, Cadbury was a natural at branding.

Fast-forward, and his company introduced Dairy Milk, its first big product brand, in 1905—and that was another imaginative leap, characteristic of branding, to link chocolate with the imagery of the dairy. Through the 20th century, Cadbury became one of the great confectionery brands, and in the 21st, it was snapped up by a conglomerate called Mondelez International.

George Cadbury helped make branding what it is today. Through huge commercial imagination, he found a new way to do the extraordinary thing that branding does—to associate an ordinary product with a larger idea, partly through what the product does, partly through what it says in its advertising, and partly through the distinctive visual style of its packaging and posters.

But, though he was a founding father of modern branding, the story goes back years, indeed centuries, before him. Cadbury's brilliant strategy was just one of a series of extraordinary creative leaps, as people have discovered new, bigger, bolder ways of using the techniques of branding. In fact, over the years, there have been five different versions of branding. The first dates back to the dawn of civilization.

Marking ownership

In the galleries of the British Museum, there's a rather delicate bronze object, found in Egypt, perhaps from near Thebes. It's not much bigger than a pen, but instead of a nib, it has a flat disk, made in a complex abstract pattern. It's 3,500 years old.

Ancient Egyptians heated up objects like this in a fire, until they were red-hot, and then used them to burn a mark on their cattle. Everyone had their own mark, and the branded sign proclaimed ownership. This particular iron has a lioness symbol, signifying that these cows belong to a temple of the goddess Sekhmet.

Branding began with fire—and the word comes from a Viking word, *brandr*, meaning 'to burn'. The link between 'brand' and 'fire' is interesting. Like fire, branding has always included a sense of excitement, of danger even, but also of warmth and comfort. You could think of the power of modern branding as the way it burns ideas into our minds. And we still talk about 'brand new', meaning straight from the fire, a phrase so familiar that our sense of 'brand' is closely connected with the idea of novelty and newness. So brands, particularly the newest, are described as 'hot'—though at the same time, oddly enough, they're also referred to as 'cool'.

Back in ancient Egypt, the branding of cattle was a clear example of branding as we see it now: using signs to give an object (a cow) deeper meaning (its ownership), in order to change people's behaviour (not stealing it) in order to create value. When invented, this practice involved a remarkable invention—making a little mark convey a big meaning—though of course it now feels completely natural. It's the earliest form, the first version, of branding.

For thousands of years, people have burned, etched, inscribed, and carved marks to attach meaning to inanimate objects—the precursor to modern branding. Builders have always etched their mark in stone, potters on ceramics, painters on cave walls. These marks say 'this is mine' or 'I made this'. The Roman empire had a logo—SPQR, Senatus Populusque Romanus, the Senate and People of Rome—which you see on coins, and inscribed in stone on Roman remains across the empire. Here, the mark has a more social meaning: 'this is ours'.

In the middle ages, the complex techniques of heraldry spread across Europe—signs that included a logo (the coat of arms) and often a slogan (the motto). Each noble family had its own mark: a mark of lineage and pedigree, a mark of membership for the family, and a mark of affiliation for all those economically intertwined with that family. And during the middle ages, the modern company started to emerge, using a trade name and often

some kind of imagery too. A handful of modern brand names date back to this time—Stella Artois, for instance, to 1366. Löwenbräu's lion symbol can be traced back to 1383.

The practice of branding had a darker side too: the burning of marks onto slaves, again to signify ownership; or onto criminals, to signify their transgression. Though we generally no longer burn marks on each other, this negative sense of 'branding' is still very common, particularly in newspaper headlines. Government policies are 'branded a failure', politicians' promises are 'branded as gimmicks', hospitals are 'branded as inadequate'.

Of course, if one farmer brands his or her animals, then very soon all farmers must do the same: so branding quickly spread and became the norm. One Texan rancher, though, became famous in the 1850s for refusing the burn marks on his cattle. His name was Samuel Maverick, and the word 'maverick', meaning someone who's stubbornly independent-minded, comes from him. Maverick explained that he didn't want to inflict pain on his cattle: others pointed out that he could claim any unmarked animal as his. Then, as now, trying to escape the system of branding was futile. Not branding is just another form of branding.

Animal branding still happens today, though often marks are frozen rather than burned. I recently saw branded horses at a stud for Lipizzaners in Transylvania, and here the complex system of marks signifies not ownership but heredity.

People, thankfully, are rarely branded, but the practice of tattooing is on the rise: a way of branding yourself, of signifying your passions, which sometimes, oddly enough, involves tattooing commercial logos like Harley-Davidson's.

And organizations still brand their property: the Rothschild family marks its estates with the family logo, and every company displays its logo on its offices, factories, and warehouses.

Guaranteeing quality

Back in the 18th century, the practice of branding property was well-established. And for craftspeople, there had been a long tradition of applying maker's marks to their work. Guilds of craftspeople used marks to try to eliminate fakes, and the law required goldsmiths and silversmiths to have their work marked by an independent 'assay office'. But with the industrial revolution, and the emergence of mass production, came a new insight: if you were a factory owner, you could put a mark not on your property, but on your *products*. You could turn a mark of provenance into an explicit mark of quality. You could morph the meaning of your mark from 'this is mine' and 'I made this' to 'this is a product you can trust'. In an era of shoddy mass-produced products, and often adulterated foods, these marks could win the trust of consumers—and command higher prices. This is the second version of branding.

The techniques of branding began to shift. Burned marks evolved into marks impressed onto products like pottery, and then into those printed onto packaging. The great pottery entrepreneur Josiah Wedgwood was a pioneer of this idea, stamping his products 'Wedgwood' from 1759 onwards. A decade later, he started adding the word 'Etruria' (the classically inspired name he gave his factory). He knew that this kind of branding could speak to the rapidly expanding middle classes, reassuring them that they were spending their hard-earned money wisely, on products that would last.

By the 1820s, the word 'brand' was being used explicitly in this new sense. The focus was on brand names and on brand reputations, and a new expertise emerged: the design of trademarks and packaging. Most of this work was done by commercial artists, now long forgotten, but occasionally companies used the work of famous

painters. Pears Soap used for many years a painting called 'Bubbles', originally entitled 'A Child's World', by John Everett Millais.

Branding gained huge new power in the 1870s, with the idea that you could protect these new assets as 'registered trademarks'. Design and law made a potent combination, and many of the earliest registered trademarks are still effective value-creators now, like Bass, Campbell's, and Kellogg's. (And it was the Bass trademark, of course, that Manet depicted in his 1882 painting, 'A Bar at the Folies-Bergère'.)

Coca-Cola started in 1886 (with, in its early days, 9 milligrams of cocaine as an ingredient), Campbell's in 1898, and Kellogg's in 1906. All, of course, are still big brands now: branding can have extraordinary longevity. All use the colour red, a colour that stands out, a colour that expresses warmth and energy—the colour of fire. And all use a typeface that resembles handwriting. They all look like signatures, like personal guarantees of quality.

By now, manufacturers routinely used advertising to promote their products, usually offering simple, functional benefits like 'delicious' and 'refreshing' for Coca-Cola. This kind of branding is designed to nurture fairly simple ideas in people's minds, mainly about quality and functionality. And this approach is still prevalent today: a famous example is the wood stain Ronseal, whose slogan has been since 1994 'It does exactly what it says on the tin'.

In fact, most branding operates in this way still: burning a name into our minds, making us remember that name, and associating the name with a limited range of mainly functional associations. For example, most household product branding works this way. And the primary meaning of a retailer brand like John Lewis (see Box 3) or Target is the quality of the products it makes or sells.

Box 3 John Lewis: happy employees

John Lewis is not just a retailer but a British institution, almost universally admired. Breaking all the rules of marketing, it aims first not for the happiness of its customers, but of its employees. And yet it's consistently voted Britain's favourite retailer. Set up in its present form by John Spedan Lewis in 1920, the company is a kind of cooperative, owned by a trust on behalf of its workers. Together, these 89,000 'partners' run over forty department stores and over 350 Waitrose supermarkets, offering exceptionally good customer service. The partners get an annual bonus, in some years as much as a fifth of salary. John Lewis's brand proposition, written by its founder back in 1925, is 'Never Knowingly Undersold'—odd English that reassures its mainly middle class shoppers that they won't find better value elsewhere. The company's secret is simple: happy staff make happy customers. Or, to put it slightly differently: branding starts from within.

Promising pleasure

But the story doesn't stop there. Around the start of the 20th century, mass production became amplified by the arrival of mass media. Factory owners realized they could combine with media owners to give their trademarks even more power. They saw that through advertising in newspapers, then cinemas and radio, they could do more than guarantee quality. They could associate their products with powerful ideas—as Cadbury did with the idea of 'purity'.

This is the kind of branding that we saw with Coca-Cola in Kenya, back at the start of this book (Figure 1), and it's another bold leap, though it seems a normal practice now. Branding could do more than guarantee quality. It could promise much bigger ideas, bolder metaphors, poetic associations: not just functional quality but also much deeper pleasure. In that way, you could create desire for things people didn't know they wanted, which would propel the sales figures, and ideally make people feel an emotional bond with, and ideally be loyal to, your brand. This is the third version of branding.

Coca-Cola, for example, moved its advertising slogan from the prosaic and functional 'delicious and refreshing' to the startlingly poetic 'ice cold sunshine' in 1932. Wheaties become 'the breakfast of champions' in 1934. And De Beers suggested that 'a diamond is forever' in 1947.

Once again, the techniques of branding shifted, into the new arts of advertising and public relations. Cultural forces like psychoanalysis played a role in this. Sigmund Freud's nephew, Edward Bernays, was a founding father of PR, and saw how we could tap into unconscious forces to manipulate people. (He thought manipulation was a good thing.)

People like Bernays saw that you could associate products with abstract ideas that went much further than the product's functional benefits. He persuaded American women to smoke cigarettes by photographing female film stars on their own on the streets of New York, linking cigarettes with a kind of private pleasure, and, even more importantly, with the idea of independence. Now, a cigarette could make you independent. An ordinary product could make you look better to others, and feel better about yourself.

Masters of branding

Advertisers started to perform this trick by defining brands through a *proposition* and a *personality*, in order to create powerfully persuasive communication. The proposition expressed the benefits the product offered consumers. Its apogee was the idea of the 'unique selling proposition', or USP, invented by the advertising agency Ted Bates in the 1940s: the concept that your advertising should communicate a benefit for the customer that was (as far as possible) unique to your product. Then a 1955 article in the *Harvard Business Review* introduced the concept of the 'brand personality', making a more emotional or subliminal appeal. Branding could now appeal to the mind and the heart, and deliberately aim to change how people think and feel.

Large manufacturers of consumer goods—Coca-Cola, Procter & Gamble, Ford, and many more—became masters of branding, and the practice began to be seen as a long-term strategic investment. The ad-man David Ogilvy's credo was that 'Every advertisement is part of the long-term investment in the personality of the brand'. Advertising was not just about selling in the short term, but about brand-building in the long term, and the advertising agencies became the champions, the guardians, the priests almost, of their clients' brands.

This version of branding turned direction, and grew in power, in the 1960s, with the arrival of television in almost every home, and of the 'creative revolution' in advertising, which produced hugely more sophisticated brand messaging, often using television as its medium. Coca-Cola no longer advertised its thirst-quenching functional powers, but its ability to make you look good to your friends, through slogans like 'The sign of good taste'. Later on, it promised to make you feel like an optimistic citizen of the world, through the famous 'I'd like to buy the world a Coke' campaign.

Bill Bernbach, at his agency Doyle Dane Bernbach, developed subtle, ironic advertising that flattered its audience's sense of their own intelligence. A famous 1959 advert for the Volkswagen Beetle shows a stark black-and-white image with a headline that reversed the received wisdom in the American car trade into the phrase 'Think small'. The advertisement is mostly white space. The headline ends with a full stop, making it sound like a definitive statement, not a sales slogan. The text is witty and knowing, spelling out all the ways that small is good (fuel consumption, parking space, price) and suggests that if you want to be different from the crowd, and smarter, then of course you'd choose a VW.

Alongside product brands, service brands started to appear: American Express, Hilton, PanAm, and many more. Naturally enough, advertisements frequently showed the people who delivered these services. Branding a service became an art in itself, more complex than branding a product. Somehow, you have to make the intangible into something people can grasp. AmEx focused on the tangible part of its service: the card itself. Others dramatized the customer's (ideal) experience. 'Halfway to Europe between cocktails and coffee', proclaimed one PanAm advert.

And building an airline brand, or a hotel brand, or a bank brand depended on getting the company's employees to do the right thing, to keep the promises made in the advertising. For the first time, branding was the job of more than just the marketing department: branding now reached across the whole company. In these ways, branding started to touch not just the product, but also the people behind it: the corporation.

Inviting belonging

Through the mid-20th century, a new force was emerging in society: the post-industrial corporation. Companies became huge supra-national centres of power. Big corporations, and their institutional investors, saw that they could broaden the impact of brand from their individual products to the company itself. This was another bold leap, and branding started to work on new audiences, beyond the consumer: on employees, investors, and opinion-formers. Companies could now be 'corporate brands', and this kind of branding could do more than promise pleasure. It could invite all kinds of stakeholder to feel a sense of belonging. By feeling they belong, employees would work harder, and customers would stay loyal for longer. This is the fourth version of branding.

The practice of branding shifted into defining an organization's purpose (or 'vision' or 'central idea'), expressing it through visual design—the logo and its supporting paraphernalia—and sharing it through the various mechanisms corporations use to build their internal working cultures. And a new kind of expert took centre-stage: the design-based brand consultant.

This concept was originally called 'corporate identity', and early pioneers included Peter Behrens at AEG in Germany before the first world war, then London Transport in the 1920s, then IBM in the 1950s. But it took off in the 1980s. Reaganism and Thatcherism glamorized the corporation still further, and created a new cohort of privatized companies—organizations like British Airways and BT. This was the golden age of the corporate.

Interestingly, at the same time, the personal computer gave individuals a new sense of power, culminating in the Apple Mac, and the 1960s generation started identifying with a new kind of apparently anti-corporate company, like Apple, Virgin, or Southwest Airlines. These new phenomena felt like consumer brands, and the old terminology of 'corporate identity' switched to 'corporate brand'—though in some ways 'uncorporate brand' would have been more appropriate.

Company v. company

Apple was a master of this art. It launched the Apple Macintosh with a famous advert, directed by Ridley Scott, which showed a female athlete (representing the Mac) running into an auditorium and throwing a sledgehammer at the Big Brother face on the screen (representing the old world of corporate computing). The advert dramatized a new kind of hip corporate brand that displaced the older model of corporate identity, epitomized by IBM. It invited consumers to belong to a movement—to help defeat 'big brother'.

These new-generation corporate brands could even expand from one industry into others, using their brand to bring their customers with them. Virgin grew from record label into airline into financial services then trains, mobile phones, and many more.

Corporate brands like Virgin appeal to consumers, but branding also became a powerful tool for companies that sell to other companies. Alongside B2C (business-to-consumer) brands, a new breed of B2B (business-to-business) brands emerged, many in the world of information technology, like Accenture, Cisco, Oracle, SAP, Goldman Sachs, 3M, and Reuters.

And it's at this point that the techniques of branding started to spread beyond the corporate world, into not-for-profits, sports clubs, political parties, cities, countries, and celebrities. More and more people talked about, and wrote about, 'brand'.

Enabling action

At the end of the 20th century, patterns of consumer behaviour were transformed by the arrival of the internet. Consumers could, as never before, become producers too. Writers like Alvin Toffler had talked about the producer-consumer, or 'prosumer', back in the 1980s, but the internet made prosumers mainstream. Suddenly, people had more knowledge and power than ever, and gained huge new scope to make and sell things, as well as buying them.

Entirely new businesses transformed industry after industry: Amazon, eBay, Google, YouTube, Skype, Facebook, Wikipedia, Airbnb, Uber. None promised pleasure, or (in any deep emotional sense) invited belonging, but they all offered people a platform on which they could do new things. They enabled action. With eBay, you could sell your stuff to the world. With YouTube, you could upload your own films, as well as exploring a giant database of video clips. With Airbnb, you could 'list your space', renting out

your home to travellers from across the planet. This is the fifth
version of branding.

These new businesses used branding not to sell but to encourage
network effects: the more people used these products, the more
useful they became. The techniques of branding therefore changed
once again. The new platforms think in terms of their role in people's
lives, and of the principles behind the user experience—and their
success depends on how well that experience works. The old arts
of advertising and logo design are much less important in this
world—and in fact most of these new brands were built without
expert logo design or advertising campaigns. Instead, the expertise
lies with the tech companies themselves, and with new kinds of
specialists like service designers.

And these platforms led to the creation of a new kind of brand, the
peer-to-peer or P2P brand: the brand of the individual seller on
eBay, or the video blogger on YouTube, or the property 'host'
on Airbnb.

Where we are now

All five versions of branding still happen, side by side. Animals
are still branded. Many of the most mundane products are still
branded for their quality and functionality. Probably the dominant
kind of branding is still the technique of giving products deeper,
more emotional associations, promising pleasure or enhanced
self-esteem—and the advertising agencies who make this happen
are still the most powerful force in the brand world. Meanwhile,
most big corporations now take their corporate brand very
seriously, and brand consultancies are still very influential.

The most recent kind of branding, version 5, is still very young.
It's impossible to predict how it will play out, and it's unclear
who the new breed of experts will be. And the story is not linear.

The start-ups behind several of the biggest internet brands have now become large global corporations, have started running brand advertisements, and have redesigned their logos to look more traditionally corporate, as we'll see in Chapter 8. They are hovering between the new kind of branding that tries to enlist participants, and the older kind that promotes a corporation.

Degrees of control

With all these different kinds of branding in play, almost anything can now be branded. What varies is the degree of control and complexity involved.

Commercial branding—of products, services, and content (such as Spider-Man or My Little Pony)—is very tightly controlled by the owners and their lawyers, and relatively simple: it helps a company sell something to a consumer, in order to extract the maximum value from the product.

Organizational branding—of companies, not-for-profits, sports clubs, political parties—is more complex. The aim is to encourage the maximum support for the organization, but that means reaching many more kinds of people (managers, employees, owners, investors, supporters, members), and is often, of necessity, less tightly controlled and policed.

Cultural branding—of places, people, movements, concepts—is the most complex of all, and may be impossible to control in any kind of corporate way. Here, the aim is to create maximum buzz around an idea, often an idea that belongs to no-one.

And the truth is that many brands straddle more than one of these worlds. IBM is a product brand, a service brand, and a corporate brand. Jamie Oliver is both a product brand and a person brand. Intel is a corporate brand and a product brand. Branding is a dynamic, opportunistic activity that constantly breaks across the conceptual categories that academics and consultants try to construct. Its role and its methods keep morphing.

B2B

Intel, in fact, is a good example of a B2B brand that broke into the B2C world too, through the 'Intel inside' campaign. Intel made advanced computer chips and sold them to computer companies, but in the late 1980s it found it hard to compete with cheaper competitors. So it started paying its customers, the computer manufacturers, to put an 'Intel inside' sticker on their products, to suggest added value. Sales of those computers rocketed. Consumers felt that 'Intel inside' conveyed quality (and an element of mystique), and Intel—though a B2B company—rapidly became famous among consumers.

Many B2B brands are now using some of the techniques of B2C branding, to appeal over the heads of their clients to their clients' customers. Airbus and Boeing sell their products to airlines, but their brands are well-known to passengers too: the latest Boeing plane can attract customers to an airline that flies it.

Traditionally, branding mattered less in the B2B world: clients bought your product or your service or your expertise, not your brand. But that's changing. Even such rational organizations as the big audit firms, like PwC and EY, now invest heavily in brand-building, not least to attract the brightest new graduates. The pioneer, in many ways, has been the consulting firm Accenture, which has invested seriously in brand-building from the day it was created, consistently using the slogan 'high performance delivered'.

The paradoxes of luxury

At the other end of the scale—where customers happily pay a huge premium for your brand—is the luxury brand. Most of the value of (say) a Ralph Lauren shirt or a Mont Blanc pen or a Cartier bag or a pair of Christian Louboutin shoes or a Ferrari car is in the brand as opposed to the product. But luxury branding, too, is on the move. Instead of selling to a few rich people in the West, these companies are selling to a vast new middle class in China. Rarity has become abundant. Many luxury businesses are broadening their appeal, for instance by collaborating with mass-market retailers: Lanvin, Versace, and Alexander Wang, for instance, with H&M; and Lemaire with Uniqlo. Burberry makes what it calls an 'entry level' perfume, cheaper than its clothes.

In the fashion industry, in fact, branding traditionally appeals to those who love labels, want to be seen wearing labels, and want to look good to their friends. But more recently it has started to work in a different way on those who are tired of labels, who avoid ostentation, or who want to feel good about themselves. So alongside the labels are the anti-labels: the newest form of branding is a very self-conscious kind of anonymity. Maison Margiela clothes often have blank labels—though the stitching of the label is visible on the outside of the garment, so they still proclaim themselves, to those in the know. New entrants like Vetements don't carry a designer name or a visible logo, and are aimed at customers who don't want to be walking adverts for brands: founder Demna Gvasalia says 'The ultimate designer, for me, is the woman who wears it'.

Wherever there's a market

What we see around us, then, is a universe of branding. Five different versions, all in play. Commercial, organizational, and cultural branding, each involving different levels of control. B2B branding, where you might think brand counts for least, and luxury branding, where it probably matters most.

Branding is also powerful in labour markets. There's tough competition for the brightest new employees, and the most compelling version 4 branding attracts the best new talent. Organizations also compete to attract finance, and a strong brand can make you more valuable to investors, and may even secure better terms from banks. Organizations increasingly work together, and this trend creates another marketplace: a strong brand can help you attract the best possible partners. Wherever there's a market, there's branding.

Is there anything that can't be branded? Are there human activities so un-corporate, so un-designed, so homespun perhaps, or so invisible, that branding could never work? Water? Air? Happiness? Even illegal products like drugs are often branded.

A constantly morphing force

We're so familiar with the idea of brand that it all seems natural to us. But branding has grown through a series of audacious leaps: from property to product, from product features to wider emotional associations, from product to organization, and from consuming to participating. Branding has expanded its scope from the commercial world, into the broader world of organizations, and then into the wide open spaces of culture. And it's exerted its power not just in the glamorous sectors you'd expect, like luxury, but also in the greyer markets of B2B. Over the years, branding has found ever more ways to change how people think, feel, and act.

Chapter 4
How branding works

Think back to how your day started today. As a consumer, you've been consuming since you woke up. You'll have made a lot of passive choices, particularly among the things you use, and the things you do by habit or default—your radio station, coffee, shower gel, phone, social media app, browser, even the company you go to work for—though at some point in the past, you made a conscious choice about all of these things. And others may be more active choices: the things you buy, your coffee shop, your lunch place. Some things, of course, you can't affect: your bus company, your computer at work.

For most of us, most of these choices are influenced at some stage by branding. We choose the cereal that tastes good, or that's nutritious, or that's cheap—but maybe also that reminds us of our childhood. We choose the radio station that best suits our mood, or gives us the most accurate news—but also that reflects who we like to think we are. We might choose the first cash machine we come across—or the one belonging to the bank we think is most ethical.

In other words, we choose things not just for functional reasons, but also because of how they make us feel about ourselves, and about our relationships with others. We make decisions based not just on the product, but also on the things that product stands for—its brand.

Brands—from Tropicana to Colgate, Illy to Shiseido, Nintendo to PowerPoint, the *New York Times* to Buzzfeed—are not just a passive phenomenon, sitting out there in the world. They get deep inside us. They are a set of ideas, feelings, memories, and images that make us do things.

Branding works on our rational brains—but also at a more profound level, on our intuitive, pre-conscious reasoning, and on our emotions. By changing how we think, and more deeply how we feel, branding changes how we act. And it reaches not just consumers, but employees too.

Branding changes how we think and feel

Through our experience with using a product, and through the messages conveyed by its advertising, we build up a set of beliefs about it. This is the rational side of branding. Aristotle, the ancient Greek philosopher, anticipated the techniques of branding in his book *Rhetoric*, and talks about this as *logos*: the word, or the rational argument. (*Logos* is also the origin of 'logo', the term we use to mean 'brand emblem'.)

For example, I've heard of Sony, I know it's a Japanese business, I know that it makes games machines, televisions, mobile phones—and also that it makes films and other forms of entertainment. I believe that its technology is good, though maybe not as advanced as (say) LG's. I think a Sony product will be well made, carefully engineered: it will be reliable and offer reasonable value for money. In these kinds of ways, branding appeals to our conscious, rational minds. It offers a 'brand proposition', and helps us calculate the benefits of buying, say, a Sony product (Figure 4). This is how branding version 2—the guarantee of quality—operates.

4. **Getting people to buy: Sony's branding changes how people think and feel about its products—and also leads them to buy, and to keep buying.**

But the real power of much modern branding is that it goes deeper. It also appeals to our intuitive, unconscious, irrational, and emotional selves. Through the pleasure a product has given us, through the memories it evokes, through the attitudes we've picked up from friends, through the storytelling in its advertising, through the colour of its logo, we build up a set of feelings. In these ways, branding creates a 'brand personality', and helps us to feel that a particular decision is right. Aristotle would probably analyse this aspect of branding as *ethos* (the character and credibility of the speaker) and *pathos* (the emotions of the audience). And this is branding version 3.

For example, I've enjoyed thousands of hours of television entertainment through Sony. In fact, it was the first television I ever bought, so to some extent I'm a Sony person. I trust Sony. Expert friends tell me that its picture quality is superior. I've seen Sony products looking good in countless films (some of them, no doubt, made by Sony Pictures). I like its communication style, and even its clunky little logo: they're understated and reassuring. These are all feelings, and writing them down like this is slightly misleading, because they exist in my mind in a pre-conscious, pre-verbal form.

Thinking fast

In fact, branding appeals very strongly to what the Nobel prize-winning scientist Daniel Kahneman calls 'system 1' thinking. He describes the differences between intuitive 'system 1' and conscious 'system 2' thinking in his book *Thinking, Fast and Slow*. We all use system 1 thinking constantly in our lives. For example, when we're driving, we don't deliberate about every gear change or every adjustment of the steering wheel: we drive largely on autopilot. Branding frequently appeals directly to our autopilot brains, getting us to pick a product on a supermarket shelf without any conscious thought. It uses logos, symbols, colours, images, music, smells, tastes to go direct to our intuitions. By creating a brand personality in people's minds, and expressing that personality through the brand's style, branding targets system 1.

Branding often works through irrational phenomena like 'habituation' and 'contagion'. For example, the *Downton Abbey* brand worked on me in both these ways, and every year I watched the programme because I always had (habituation) and because so many other people did (contagion). As human beings, we're subject to a whole range of cognitive biases like these, and branding often depends on them. There's even a cognitive bias, recognized by social psychologists, called 'the IKEA effect', which is our tendency to feel attached to things just because we've assembled them.

Habituation is an important contributor to the goal of brand loyalty—one of the aims of branding versions 3 and 4. And contagion is vital in branding version 5. Many online businesses depend on network effects: the more users a service like Airbnb or Uber has, the more useful it becomes. Here, the interplay of functional and emotional is critical. 'Contagion' becomes a complex thing, and I chose Airbnb, for example, not just because so many other people do, but also because it benefits me to behave like them.

Most branding, in fact, gets its power by mixing the intuitive and the rational. Sometimes, branding has an automatic, intuitive effect first (system 1 thinking), and then we post-rationalize (system 2). In the supermarket, I might unthinkingly grab a bar of Green and Black's chocolate because I'm drawn subliminally to the sophisticated, dark packaging. I'll then tell myself I chose it because it's healthily organic.

At other times, branding starts with a purely functional appeal, but as we get used to it, we tell people about it, we feel warmer towards it, and it gains emotional dimensions. For example, the discount supermarkets Aldi and Lidl took off by simply being cheap, but they became brands that Britain's middle classes now feel proud to identify with. Offering your dinner-party guests a bottle of Aldi wine shows just what a savvy shopper you are.

Inside the brain

Some experts use brain science to analyse the interplay between rational and irrational. They believe that decisions get made first in those primitive parts of our brains that we inherit from our reptilian predecessors. We then justify them in our limbic brain, the part that deals with our social feelings, or in our cortex, where we do our rational thinking. So, for example, I might buy a gas-guzzling SUV car—let's say a Porsche Cayenne. I tell myself that I chose the Porsche because it's practical for driving down muddy lanes to my country cottage: that's the cortex at work, post-rationalizing. I tell friends I bought it because the high driving position makes it safer for other road users: that's the limbic system, making me a good citizen. But the real reason remains a secret, buried in my reptilian brain: I chose it because it gives me a primitive sense of power.

More precisely, the new field of 'consumer neuroscience' is starting to show how branding works inside the brain. It uses machines called functional magnetic resonance imaging (or 'fMRI') scanners to watch how brains respond to stimuli. Scientists have looked to see the effects of branding stimuli (to being shown a logo, for example, or given a branded fizzy drink). There's evidence that branding produces activity in the ventromedial prefrontal cortex, which sits behind the forehead, and is associated with feelings of reward. Tasted blind, Coca-Cola and Pepsi do this equally, but when people can see the cans, Coca-Cola seems to produce this activity much more than Pepsi does.

Branding also produces activation in the hippocampus, much deeper inside the brain, and in the dorsolateral prefrontal cortex. Both these areas are associated with memory. So branding seems to stimulate brain activity to do with reward and memory. All this is interesting, but unsurprising: it tells us where things happen in the brain but not why they happen. And it's based on what people do in the highly artificial surroundings of the fMRI lab. We have a long way to go before we can understand branding at the level of brain cells.

Branding changes how we act

So how does all of this influence people's behaviour? Obviously enough, branding gets us, as consumers, to buy. Uniqlo's branding, for instance, makes us *think* that its products offer good design at an amazing price. The branding also makes us *feel* things: perhaps that we like Uniqlo's slightly quirky, but also very neat and tidy, Japanese ethos. And so we *act*: we buy this t-shirt (and, probably, half a dozen other impulse purchases as we go round the store).

But there's more. Branding attracts more customers in. It gets them to buy more things. It gets them to buy things from you more often. It gets people to buy things in new ways. In the field of music, for example, the Apple brand got us to switch from CDs to downloads, and then the Spotify brand got people to switch from downloads to streaming. And in many cases—again, Apple is a good example—it gets people to pay more, to pay a 'brand premium'.

If you're a charity like Oxfam, branding gets people to donate to you. If you created a television show like *The Good Wife*, it gets people to watch it. Even if your service is (apparently) free, like Twitter, it gets people to use it. And good branding can get retailers to sell your product, comparison sites to push it, agents and brokers to favour it—all of which propels sales.

Branding, then, gets people to buy—which means that good branding, one way or another, increases the company's revenue.

But the really deep power of branding is that it gets us to keep doing things, into the future. Brands burn themselves into our minds. They create not a single act, but habitual behaviour. Branding gets people not just to *buy* you, but to *buy into* you: not just to pay money, but also to make an emotional investment. As a result, in the words of the branding expert Tim Ambler, 'a brand is an upstream reservoir of future cashflow'. Good branding makes your future more predictable.

To take a specific example, Toyota in recent years has had a spate of quality problems, which has forced it to recall cars for repair. But Toyota's branding helps it survive. Customers believe that, in spite of recent faults, these are good cars. People like Toyota's rather serious brand personality. And so they buy Toyota again.

Indeed, Toyota still sells nine million cars a year, even after several major product recalls.

This kind of commitment is conscious and deliberate, but branding also creates a less deliberate behavioural commitment: we often buy the same brand of (say) ketchup out of mere habit.

So branding gets people outside the organization to keep buying, and often to recommend the product to friends. It can turn customers into unofficial salespeople. It can even, in some cases, encourage them to get together in 'brand communities'—groups of fans. These brand communities seem to form particularly around products that are toys, either for adults or children. Harley Davidson, JEEP, Barbie, and LEGO all have fan groups, official and unofficial.

Good branding gets the media to praise you, policy-makers to support you, and perhaps even gets regulators to smooth your path. And it gets investors to stay with you, through bad times as well as good.

All of this means that, in financial language, your 'risk' goes down: your future is more secure. Through the downturn following the 2008 crash, the market value of America's largest companies declined dramatically. But if you look instead at the value of just the companies with the most valuable brands, their performance dipped much less. They also returned to growth by the summer of 2009—almost three years before their less well-branded rivals. If you have a big brand, you recover much faster, and your risks are therefore much lower.

Loyalty is for dogs

This kind of consumer commitment is often called 'brand loyalty'. But loyalty, when you analyse it, is a complex thing. It can be a matter of attitude, or a matter of behaviour, or both. Sometimes people are both attitudinally and behaviourally loyal: I have to admit that I both love, and keep buying, Apple. In cases like this, brand experts often talk about 'brand love' and even 'lovemarks'— and these kinds of consumer are the true 'brand fans'. But there are limits. Though some of us may feel something akin to love towards one or two brands, very few have room in our hearts to love more than one or two. Brand love will always be the exception rather than the rule.

As consumers get more and more choices, and become better informed about what's on the market, they tend to become less loyal. Many people now do some of their shopping at premium supermarkets, and some at discount stores: they're too canny to be loyal to one or the other. In the supermarket, shoppers often choose the store's own-label products over the traditional branded ones. Most of us carry a stack of 'loyalty' cards from various stores and hotel groups. We're not really loyal to any of them, we just make multiple, and partial, commitments. As someone once ruefully said, 'loyalty is for dogs'. A study by the management consultants EY in 2012 suggested that only 40 per cent of consumers worldwide buy things out of brand loyalty, and only 25 per cent in the USA.

Waitrose is my favourite supermarket, and I'd always recommend it to people, but in practice I shop at all the main supermarkets. I'm attitudinally, but not behaviourally, loyal. The brand expert Byron Sharp suggests that the market is now dominated by promiscuous consumers like me. These people may *feel* loyal to, say, Dell, but they actually buy Lenovo or Asus. He calls them 'loyal switchers'.

In other cases, people stick with a product even though they don't like it. It's hard to switch bank, for instance, so most consumers are behaviourally but not attitudinally loyal. We use the same broadband, the same browser, the same search engine, and probably the same online retailer day after day, without loving any of them. In these cases, consumers are 'habitual users'.

So branding today, while aiming ideally to create brand fans, knows that in most cases its best result will be loyal switchers or habitual users. Yet these kinds of half-loyalty are still complex commitments to brands—and branding still helps reduce the risk of losing customers.

The pay-off of branding

In the 1980s, two writers, David Aaker and Kevin Lane Keller, wanted to describe more precisely these powerful effects of branding. They developed the concept of 'brand equity', by which they mean the value of a brand—of the ideas out there in people's minds—to the company. Specifically, a product's brand equity is the additional value it can create, compared with a similar product with fewer or no associations in people's minds. Keller describes it as 'the added value a product accrues as a result of past investments in the marketing activity for the brand'. The goal of branding, then, is to maximize brand equity.

For example, I can go to a pharmacy and buy ibuprofen from a company called Value Health, and it costs me 35p. Value Health means nothing to me: it's an anonymous manufacturer, not a brand. Next to it on the shelf is a product called Nurofen. It has the same active ingredient, but it's also a brand, owned by Reckitt Benckiser. Nurofen has been built up over the years through millions of pounds of advertising. And Nurofen costs £2. The price difference hints at Nurofen's brand equity—the brand is so powerful that the retailer can charge £1.65 extra per pack.

That's a simple case, but brand equity is often more complex. In the case of a low-cost airline, or a discounter supermarket, the price is actually lower: brand equity for IndiGo or Lidl comes from not a price premium but greater sales volumes or faster growth. And equity may not always be about money. A brand's equity, or its relative advantage, could be measured in longevity, growth rates, or even social impact.

Aaker analyses brand equity into three components, brand awareness, brand associations, and brand loyalty. Brand *awareness* is the most basic: people's level of familiarity with the product or organization. Brand *associations* are all those other ideas and feelings—the ideas people associate with, for example, IKEA—that make people choose to buy, or not to buy, including importantly the product's perceived quality. And brand *loyalty* is the pinnacle: people's feelings of commitment to a particular product or organization—the greater the commitment, the less the company has to spend on marketing.

Keller takes the thinking a stage further, labelling his version 'customer-based brand equity'. Keller starts with *salience*. For Zara, for example, this would mean 'I've heard of Zara, and when I think of fashion, Zara is top-of-mind'. Then he talks about the product's meaning, divided into *performance* ('Zara clothes are well made and low priced') and *imagery* ('Zara is Spanish, on trend, fast fashion, and for people like me').

Up another level is the customer's response, divided into *judgements* ('it's good quality, I prefer it to Primark, I'd always look in there') and *feelings* ('I feel excited about Zara, it makes me look good, I feel good about myself'). And at the top, much like Aaker's loyalty, is *resonance* ('I feel loyal to Zara, I always shop there, I'm a Zara fan').

Keller visualizes all this as a pyramid, with 'salience' at the base and 'resonance' at the peak. This is probably the most widely used diagram by brand academics, and it's been adapted for use by many brand-owning companies too.

Brand equity can be strong or weak. Indeed, you can have negative brand equity. This happens when a branded product gets sold for less than its generic or own-label equivalent, or when no-one will buy it at all. In 1991, Gerald Ratner, chief executive of his family jewellery business, joked that his stores' earrings were 'cheaper than an M&S prawn sandwich but probably wouldn't last as long', and his comment immediately sent the Ratners brand into negative equity.

Branding on the inside

So branding builds (we hope) positive brand equity. It appeals to consumers, in both the short term and the long term. That's all obvious. And many writers on branding leave it here. They talk about the need to take consumers up a 'ladder' or through a 'funnel' from brand awareness to preference to loyalty.

But less visible is the internal effect of branding: it operates too on the people behind the brand, the employees. In a branded organization, people are normally strongly aware of the brand they work for. At a place like GE, where, as we've seen, the brand is officially about 'imagination at work', they might think about bringing their imagination to work, they might feel that they like this spirit of inventiveness, going right back to GE's founder, Thomas Edison. And so they work hard to invent. That, at least, is the theory.

Branding gets good recruits to apply to, and join, the organization. The glamour of the brand brings new employees in, and though the reality is usually more mundane and imperfect, the brand sustains them. Once inside, it can focus people's efforts, so that they work harder. It can help people feel more united, and so collaborate with their colleagues, rather than fighting them. Branding can make people feel more positive, more 'engaged', to use the management jargon—and in fact there's a whole sub-set of branding called 'employer branding'. The result is that there's less effort to hire people, fewer mistakes in hiring, more productive workers, less wasted effort, less internal conflict or duplication of work.

And branding can work not just on employees but also on others who help the company produce what it produces: banks, for example, and suppliers. A strong brand, for instance, makes you more attractive to your bank and could help you negotiate lower interest rates. And it can certainly extract the best possible prices from your suppliers, who are keen to be associated with your brand.

In all these ways, branding can make the organization much more efficient—which means that costs go down.

For insiders too, the brand has effects which last into the future. In a business like Google, the brand encourages people not just to do today's job, but to help create tomorrow's success. It's the thing you have to live up to. Google's brand is about organizing the world's information, and its view, in Eric Schmidt's words, is that 'big problems are information problems'. Everything—education, healthcare, transport, finance, crime—is soluble by data, so as a Googler you're constantly challenged to use data to solve a new big problem (and so create a new big business). Branding can encourage people inside their organizations to grow, in lots of ways: at a minimum, to stay with the company, to learn new skills, to develop new methods, to invent new products, to expand into new markets.

All of which means that good branding helps employees to maximize the organization's future opportunities.

A corporate asset

So branding works on us at a rational level, changing how we think; and more deeply at an intuitive and emotional level, changing how we feel. It affects our knowledge of products and our judgements about them; but it also affects our feelings, sensations, and memories. And in these ways, it changes how we act—both our conscious purchasing decisions, and our autopilot reflexes in the supermarket.

Branding affects the behaviour not just of consumers, but of employees too. And the results are not just short-term blips but long-term patterns that last into the future.

In the short term, good branding increases revenues and decreases costs, which generates profit. In the long term, it minimizes risk and maximizes opportunity, which leads to long-term growth prospects. Combine profit with growth, and you get commercial value. So brand is amazingly powerful commercially, and as we saw in Chapter 1, for many organizations, their brand is their biggest asset.

But there's another dimension too. Not-for-profit organizations have always aimed at a different kind of value, social rather than commercial. And many corporations are now aiming at both. It's possible to analyse social value in the same way as commercial value, from the consumer and the employee perspective, looking for short-term and long-term effects. We'll explore the idea of social value in Chapter 7.

Secrets of success

So branding, at its best, creates huge value. But what exactly does successful branding look like? Some brands, like Johnson & Johnson, have an ethical impact, holding the company to generally high standards. Some brands lead through engineering, like Dyson or Huawei (see Box 4); others through customer service, like Nordstrom or John Lewis. Some score on recognizability: Mastercard, for instance, is visible and distinctive everywhere. Others, like Stella Artois—almost 700 years old—simply last longer. Douwe Egberts dates back to 1753, C&A to 1841, and Levi's to 1850.

Yet, of course, brands fail too. Businesses like Arthur Andersen or the *News of the World* are accused of malpractice, so their brands become tainted in people's minds, and they no longer attract

customers. Others, like Blackberry, Borders, or Woolworth,
get to feel old or irrelevant. Some, like Blockbuster, Kodak, and
Polaroid, get overtaken by technology. Companies with good
brands can make terrible mistakes and survive. Tylenol hit a
crisis in 1982 when seven people in Chicago died after taking
capsules that turned out to contain cyanide. But the brand was
so strong that, only six months later, sales had returned to
normal. Hoover ran a disastrous promotional competition in
1992, which forced it to give away £50 million of free airline
flights. The business was sold, but the brand continues. And
failing brands can come back to life. The fashion company
Burberry restored its fortunes by reinventing its original design
principles in contemporary ways, making pioneering use of
digital technology and social media—and in that clever way
rebuilt its brand. The Nokia brand has lived through several
cycles of decline and revival. The Moleskine and Polaroid
brands have been revived by new owners. Indeed, to borrow the

name of yet another durable brand, you could say that brands themselves are like Teflon: bad news seems not to stick to them for long.

So what's the secret of success? Sadly, there's no neat formula, no guaranteed method. But common sense, and my own experience in branding, suggest three themes.

First, successful branding stands out. Great brands are different. The companies behind them do their own thing, rather than copying others. Southwest Airlines pioneered low-cost point-to-point air travel. LEGO is not like other toys. No other shoe company is quite like TOMS, the company that, for every pair it sells, donates a pair to an impoverished child. The online eyewear retailer Warby Parker has a similar programme. Rather than just meeting existing consumer needs, great branding tends to lead the market: Chobani, Tesla, and Tencent have all brought new things to people. The best branding is radical, and its ideas are big. But the companies behind the greatest brands are not necessarily the inventors of new technologies. Like Apple or Sky (in very different ways), they're the popularizers.

Which leads to the second theme: great branding belongs to all of us. It's simple enough to be widely understood and shared, and to become part of everyday culture. Indeed, it may sometimes help lead and shape that culture. Great branding comes naturally to the companies that do it: it's authentic, human, and not corporate or mechanistic. It's easy to understand, share, and even join in. For the British middle classes, John Lewis is a great example of branding that's easy to like and easy to spread. The best branding is social, and its ideas are simple.

And to become a social property like that, to be credible, successful branding does what it says. Great brands are built on reality, not mere image. The Indian airline IndiGo promises to be on time, and is. BP, on the other hand, promised to go 'beyond petroleum' and didn't, which damaged its brand. Successful companies know how to mobilize their people to keep their brand promise, day after day—which often means keeping this as simple as possible. The best branding is tangible, and its ideas are true.

For all three of these reasons, successful branding depends on strong leadership. It happens through conviction, rather than consensus—that's the only route to simplicity. It depends on substance: not just a nice logo, but a thoughtful design of the whole customer experience. And, like everything else in life, it also depends on luck: being in the right place with the right product at the right time.

Branding by numbers

So branding aims to build brand equity, and more widely to create commercial and social value. How can all this be measured? Broadly, you can measure three things: how people think and feel, how they act, and the value that's created.

Measuring the thoughts and feelings in people's minds is traditionally done through surveys and focus groups. Big brand-owners commission market research themselves, or buy into databases like Y&R's BrandAsset Valuator, which is constantly surveying thousands of consumers about thousands of famous brands. Many use a very simple measure called the 'net promoter score', which asks people how likely they are to recommend your brand. The maximum score is 100, and the minimum is minus 100. A brand with very committed customers, like Apple, usually scores around 60.

Measuring behaviour means tracking data like customer numbers, frequency of purchase, repeat buying, overall sales, and market share. More recently, companies have started measuring online behaviour such as Facebook likes and Twitter re-tweets. These measurements are more objective than brand perceptions, but harder to interpret: it's often very hard to say how much of this month's sales growth, for instance, is actually the result of branding activity.

Some companies go a stage further, and try to measure the value that all this behaviour creates. They aim to put a dollar value on their brand, based on its ability to generate future revenues. Every year, four organizations—Interbrand, BrandZ, Brand Finance, and *Forbes* magazine—produce league tables of brand valuations. Currently, the most valuable brands are, unsurprisingly, technology brands, like Apple, Google, Microsoft, and IBM. The numbers are astonishingly high. In 2016, BrandZ valued the Google brand, for example, at $229 billion, which was roughly the GDP of Portugal. But this is not a precise science—the four different firms produce wildly different valuations—and you only get a truly accurate measure of your brand's value (as with the value of your house) if you sell it to someone.

The many dimensions of brand impact

These measures tend to focus on the external and commercial impacts of branding. But increasingly, as we've seen, businesses are interested in the effect of branding on employees, and also on its potential to achieve social benefits. So new, broader measurement techniques are emerging, such as the 'MeaningfulBrands' index produced by Havas Media.

And it's this multi-dimensional impact that accounts for the world's current fascination with branding. Branding changes how people think, feel, and act, in both the short term and the long term, both inside and outside the organization. And it creates value, both commercial and social.

It's a big job, and creating all these effects depends on whole armies of people. The footsoldiers in those armies are the people known as 'brand managers'.

Chapter 5
The branding business

On 13 May 1931, deep inside Procter & Gamble—a giant consumer-goods company—a junior marketing manager called Neil McElroy wrote a memo that launched the whole branding business. McElroy was in charge of Camay soap, which was performing less well than P&G's other soap brands like Ivory. So McElroy proposed that every P&G brand should have what he called a 'brand man'. The brand man, supported by a specialist team, would push that product's sales, using things like market research, advertising, and packaging design. That way, every brand would get the attention it deserved. McElroy's proposal was adopted, and 'brand management' was born. McElroy then rose through the ranks of P&G, and eventually, strangely enough, became the US Secretary of Defense. Or perhaps it's not so strange. Perhaps the essence of the brand manager's role is to defend their brand in the great war of commerce.

McElroy's memo invented a completely new job: the brand manager. And brand managers have become the central players in the business of branding. They almost always work inside the company's marketing department. Under them, or alongside them, are people working on all the other marketing activities: market research and analytics, marketing strategy, marketing communications (including advertising, PR, social media, sponsorship, and media planning), and product development.

Nowadays, though, branding goes miles beyond the marketing department, and depends on many more people than just the marketing team people, so brand managers influence, orchestrate, and coach their colleagues right across the organization.

Some of the time, these people aim to build brands scientifically, by collecting as much data as possible, by understanding what triggers people's behaviour, by experimenting with alternative methods, and by deploying the techniques that work. But human behaviour is almost impossible to pin down. It's hard to turn branding into a formula, and branding therefore depends also on creativity: on imagination, intuition, going beyond the evidence, and making something new. The business of branding is part science, part art—but in the end, art matters more.

Not always what it seems

Behind the brands we know and love (or hate) are the millions of companies that own them: the manufacturers, service companies, media businesses, and so on, where all these brand managers work. And not just commercial companies but other kinds of organization: not-for-profits, schools, government bodies, museums, political parties, cities, countries, celebrities.

But beneath all the familiar names, all is not what it seems. In consumer goods—the original home of branding—most brands are actually owned by a much larger organization, like Nestlé, Pepsico, and Procter & Gamble. Dove and Ben & Jerry's, for example, belong to Unilever. Pringles belongs to Kellogg's. Whiskas belongs to Mars. Cadbury and Kenco belong to Mondelez International. Braun and Ariel belong to Procter & Gamble. Innocent Drinks is 90 per cent owned by the Coca-Cola Company. These and many other famous names look like companies in their own right, but are actually just properties of a handful of mega-corporations.

Going in the other direction, some brands that look as though they belong to a single giant organization are actually run by dozens of smaller companies. They operate under the protective umbrella of a big brand name, through franchising and licensing. Of all the McDonald's restaurants worldwide, 85 per cent are actually a smaller company operating a franchise. Most of the big chain hotels are owned by local property companies who use the brand name under licence. Virgin appears to be one thing, but is actually 400 separate companies. A few, like Virgin Galactic, are wholly owned by Virgin Group. Most are companies that Virgin part-owns. Some, like Virgin Media, are separate businesses that use the Virgin name under licence. In PwC, the accounting and consulting giant, each of the 159 national partnerships is a separate legal entity which through a legal arrangement is licensed to use the PwC brand.

So behind the brands we encounter every day, there's a much less visible, and much more complex, pattern of ownership. Brands, in other words, are themselves products that can be bought and sold, borrowed and lent.

Managing or leading

The scope and power of the brand manager varies hugely from organization to organization. In a business-to-business company, or a not-for-profit organization, branding may be a relatively unimportant, tactical tool, and the brand manager normally sits a long way down the hierarchy, with a small team and little power. Their role is limited to managing communications or policing design.

But in consumer goods companies, in retailers, and in luxury products most of all, branding is central to the organization's success. Branding is seen as a strategic activity, encompassing all the ways the organization touches its customers. The brand team is usually large and powerful, and brand gets talked about a lot at the top of the business.

Many organizations now realize that branding can no longer be seen as just a sub-set of marketing: indeed, it's the other way round, and marketing is a sub-set of branding. Some companies, like Mattel, McDonald's, and Procter & Gamble, have created a new role, chief brand officer, which encompasses both traditional branding and some of the other functions, such as innovation and customer service, that are vital to brand-building.

And in some organizations, the only place where all those roles meet is the CEO. Particularly in those companies that believe in the internal power of branding, alongside its influence on outside consumers, many chief executives today see themselves as the steward of their organization's brand (or brands)—as, in a sense, the ultimate brand manager.

The writer David Aaker makes a distinction between tactical 'brand management' and the much broader, more strategic concept of 'brand leadership'. In his view, brand management has a short-term perspective, setting out to create the best possible brand image in the consumer's mind. Its impact is measured (if at all) in sales and market share. Brand leadership has a much more strategic perspective, aiming to maximize brand equity, juggling a whole portfolio of products, focusing on the employees too, and driven by a very clear statement of what the company wants its brand to stand for. You could go further and say that brand management polices the world as it is: it's mainly a top–down, process-heavy control mechanism. Brand leadership, in contrast, tries to shape the world as it could be: it's more a lateral, experimental, creativity tool. Brand management focuses on individual products; brand leadership aims to use the brand idea to direct the whole organization.

Brand-led or not?

How many organizations are brand-led in this way, adopting an approach the academics call 'brand orientation'? CEOs differ in their views on this subject. Richard Reed, founder of Innocent Drinks, declares that 'the brand is the business, the business is the brand'. Sometimes, as with Innocent, the brand-led philosophy started because the CEO had a marketing background, but often—as in many continental European organizations—it was more cerebral in spirit. And often CEOs elevate the brand concept into the grander notion of 'purpose'.

But others see brand as just one of many factors in their business life, and see it not as the driver but as the consequence of good decision-making. Some commercial organizations hold the idea of branding at arm's length. Dyson likes to say that it's an engineering business, not a marketing operation. Ryanair says it's too pragmatic for airy-fairy big ideas. Others feel that the excitement of branding has passed. Until recently, it was the biggest source of intangible value for many organizations, but now there are other contenders, such as the customer data they hold.

The truth is that practice varies, and organizations hold different views—deep enough perhaps to be called 'theologies'. Some adopt brand leadership, where the brand identity is seen as a strategic asset, used constantly in decision-making, and shaping innovation. Others are driven by more commercial or pragmatic objectives. Some manage their brand explicitly, others rely on creating an implicit climate. Some control everything from the top, others allow much more freedom. Some push relentlessly to be consistent, others welcome variation and innovation.

Philosopher and coach

So the organization may be brand-led or brand-supported. And the brand manager may be a lowly functionary, or a senior marketing person, or one of the new breed of 'chief brand officers', or even occasionally the CEO. But whatever their status, their role—the task of brand management—is changing.

The role used to be relatively easy to define: writing the brand strategy, achieving consistency in the branding work, policing every piece of design, and tracking the brand's performance. But the scope of branding in many organizations is much less clear-cut than it was twenty years ago. At one moment, big long-term questions of meaning and purpose are central to the CEO, while at the next moment, the pressure shifts to short-term results, and branding is little more than a sales gadget. Brand managers therefore increasingly have to hold the high ground, to remind their CEO of the long-term value to be derived from investing in the brand. They argue for the importance of values, meanings, and ideas in the minds of consumers—and of employees too. Often it's the head of brand who is reminding the organization's leaders how critical it is to building purpose, confidence, conviction, and unity among employees. Their current keyword is 'purpose', which has more currency for many chief executives than 'brand'. As the champions of meaning and purpose, and the posers of 'why' questions, brand managers are almost the *philosophers* of their organizations.

At the same time, the reach of brand managers is widening. When branding was essentially about communicating, the job could be done within the brand department. But increasingly, customers believe deeds not words: the whole customer experience, rather than the latest advertising campaign. And this means influencing colleagues in many other departments, including product design, engineering, and customer service. Many organizations, as we've seen, are keen to build the right brand in the minds of employees, just as much as among consumers. They use branding to change how employees think, feel, and act. Often, they produce a set of guidelines for how employees should behave—even in meetings that no consumer will ever see.

So the brand manager's task becomes an educational one. In some cases, this means teaching the whole organization to collectively deliver the best possible customer experience, in order to build the right brand for consumers. In others, it goes even further, and means building the right brand for employees too, getting them to 'live the brand'. To control communications, brand managers used to deploy brand manuals and guidelines. Now, they're much more likely to talk about practical tools and online learning. The brand manager has become, in effect, the organization's *coach*—its teacher and trainer—using an array of educational media and practical toolkits.

Scientist and creative director

Today, brand managers are also learning the habits of the *scientist*. This is because CEOs increasingly demand 'scientific' data from their marketing people—not just impressions and instincts but evidence and quantification—to justify their budgets. Brand managers are therefore getting interested in a range of new scientific disciplines. As we saw in Chapter 4, consumer neuroscience is still too young to be of much practical use. There's an emerging science called computational aesthetics, which aims to be able to predict which designs will work best just by measuring their features (line widths, curve angles, colours, brightnesses, and so on)—but that's still a long way behind the effectiveness of the human eye.

But another kind of data—often described as 'big data'—now plays a central role in branding. Much of what a company does in the market—communicating, selling, and delivering its product or service—now happens online, which means it gets tracked, which means there's data about it. Big data can tell a brand manager which online campaigns get most clicks, which tweets get most re-tweets, which discounts work best, which sales channels are most efficient, who the customers are, where they are, what else they like, how much they use your product, and what they say about it on Facebook.

Using this data, the brand manager's goal is to build a brand that's ahead of people's changing needs. Ford, for instance, is monitoring its customers' driving habits from its R&D centre in Silicon Valley. Big data can help you identify new trends and new needs, for example by analysing what people are searching for on Google. Big data can help you get pricing right, and to experiment with new products. And of course it can help you target communication at exactly the right people—for example, showing people advertising based on what they've been writing about in their emails. This kind of personalized brand-building is now commonplace—and so easy to do that brand-owners worry about 'the creep factor', the tendency for consumers to feel intruded on by brands that know too much about their lives—and therefore to reject the companies that do that.

So brand people are increasingly becoming data scientists. In fact, in many companies, the marketing department is now the biggest buyer of IT. The only trouble with big data is that it's big—there's far too much of it for it to be quickly useful. A 2013 IBM study suggested that 40 per cent of companies don't yet have the tools to understand all this data.

And the truth is that branding will always depend on creativity. Branding now depends as never before on innovation: constantly offering the next flavour, the latest store format, the newest technology. Brands that don't change die—in other words, companies have to keep trying to update the ideas about them in people's minds. Steve Jobs used to quote his favourite Bob Dylan line: 'he not busy being born is busy dying'. Many brand managers therefore focus on stimulating the organization to constantly renew itself. They push for rapid experimentation, and they often try and speed up the organization's body clock. Indeed, it's often the brand manager's role to push for renewal—to be the organization's *creative director*.

So brand managers today are a fascinating combination of philosopher, coach, scientist, and creative director.

Bringing in experts

In a few companies—Burberry is a good example—the brand managers do all this branding work in-house. And there are signs that others are moving in this direction: design, for example, is being brought in-house at places like IBM. But to increase their chances of success, most brand managers rely on outside agencies—advertising agencies, design consultancies, PR companies, and so on. Often, an agency works for a company for far longer than any individual brand manager or marketing director: the agency becomes the fount of knowledge, the keeper of the brand.

Originally, brand managers hired advertising and public relations agencies to get the message out. The advertising business dates back well into the 19th century (J. Walter Thompson, for instance, was founded way back in 1864) and PR began in the early 20th century, with Edward Bernays, who we met in Chapter 3, as one of its founding fathers.

These pioneers, working in the age of scientific management, often saw themselves as scientists. J. Walter Thompson set up its own 'University of Advertising' and worked closely with the psychologist John B. Watson, founder of the behaviourist school. There was a belief that you could study, understand, and then control human behaviour, however irrational it might be.

In this scientific spirit, brand managers felt the need to understand their customers better, and the market research business grew to meet that need. One of its founders was George Gallup, who started his business in 1935. Over the years, they developed a range of techniques, 'quantitative' (surveys), and 'qualitative' (focus groups). More recently, market research has focused on what consumers do, rather than what they say they'll do, using 'ethnographic' techniques (observing people's behaviour), and analysing 'big data' on their buying behaviour. Some neither talk to nor observe consumers: instead they use the techniques of semiotics to analyse the cultural artefacts—films, music, design—that surround consumers and shape their lives.

Buying creativity

At the same time, brand managers brought in design and brand agencies to create or renew their 'brand identity' or 'look and feel'. Initially, they used packaging design companies, and then—as branding spread from the branding of products into the branding of companies—they worked with corporate identity companies, of which Landor, founded in 1941, was one of the first.

By the 1960s, these design companies, together with the proponents of the new 'creative revolution' in advertising, had tipped the balance away from science towards art. Brand managers no longer attempted to control consumer behaviour, but to stimulate it through the power of imagination, in graphic design, photography, illustration, film-making, and copywriting.

These advertising, PR, market research, and design agencies dominated the scene until the 21st century, when the digital revolution changed everything. Brand managers had to quickly master the digital world, and 'digital agencies' emerged, of many different kinds, from advertising agencies specializing in online advertising, like AKQA, R/GA, and SapientNitro, to 'search engine marketing' companies that helped make sure that people searching on Google would find you.

At the same time, brand managers needed to design more than just their brand identity. To shape how their customers saw their brand, they had to get the whole customer experience right, particularly the online experience. The product design company IDEO moved into this area, joined by specialist service design businesses like Livework and Foolproof. 'Experience design' became one of the hottest buzz-phrases in the branding business.

Meanwhile, increasingly sceptical consumers became less interested in sales talk and more interested in broader 'content', through corporate blogs, social media, and magazines, and 'content marketing' agencies emerged to create all this material, like Redwood and Cedar (both, oddly, named after trees).

Media, which used to be very simple (television, radio, press, posters), became, in the digital world, very complex, and 'media agencies' (formerly the least exciting departments of advertising agencies) became big and powerful agencies in their own right. Specialists like Mindshare or OMD were the people who knew enough to get your content to the right people at the right time, using the right channels, at the best possible price. The scientists had returned.

The big four

These forces hugely multiplied the number of agencies on the scene, but at the same time agencies were consolidating too. Just as the world's big consumer brands had clustered into companies like Procter & Gamble and Unilever, so the agencies started to cluster into groups big enough to serve them. Four giant groups— Interpublic, Omnicom, Publicis, and WPP—now dominate the industry.

The biggest, and best known, is WPP, built from scratch by the British entrepreneur Martin Sorrell. Bizarrely, WPP stands for Wire and Plastic Products: its original business was making wire shopping baskets. Sorrell bought the company in 1985 as a platform on which to build an empire of marketing agencies. Within a few years, he had bought two advertising giants, J. Walter Thompson and Ogilvy, and the group now employs 120,000 people. It includes advertising agencies like JWT and Ogilvy; brand agencies like

Brand Union and Landor; the market research company Kantar; the digital agency AKQA; and the media agency GroupM.

While Sorrell was shaping WPP in London, three US-based advertising agencies merged to form another giant called Omnicom, which is now WPP's biggest rival. Omnicom has three large advertising agencies, all with rather anonymous initials as their names: DDB, BBDO, and TBWA. Over the years, the group has also bought brand agencies (such as Interbrand and Wolff Olins), market research specialists Flamingo, content company Redwood, media agency OMD, and many more: around 70,000 people now work for Omnicom.

WPP and Omnicom have two slightly smaller competitors. The French group Publicis has around 60,000 people, with agencies like BBH and Saatchi & Saatchi. And Interpublic, also US-based, has 50,000 people: its most famous agencies are McCann-Erickson and FutureBrand.

Generally, clients interact with individual companies in these groups, rather than with the group itself. The groups need to maintain the separate identities of these member firms in order to attract creative people, and also to minimize client conflicts. But WPP pulls them together frequently, to serve big clients like Vodafone jointly. Omnicom has a consortium called Team Nissan to serve one of its biggest clients. The trend across the industry is probably towards closer collaboration.

Alongside the big groups, there are still thousands of independent agencies, with more starting up every year. Consolidation and fragmentation happen side-by-side.

Life in an agency

In most of these agencies, the most visible people are the account managers, sometimes called 'client services'. Their role is to make

5. Inside the brand business: ideas are developed jointly by clients and consultants in creative sessions, like this workshop at the brand consultancy Wolff Olins.

the best possible working relationship between client and agency, meeting clients' needs, and keeping clients happy. Behind the scenes, they also have to keep the agency's own team happy, and to make sure their work is done on time and to budget. In design and brand agencies, where the focus may be less on the relationship and more on the work, these people may be called project or programme managers (Figure 5).

Alongside the account managers are consultants, sometimes called strategists or planners. Their job is to make sure that the agency's branding advice achieves its client's business objectives. They'll speak business language (up to a point, at least), and use PowerPoint and Excel. Some will focus on the client's organization, and facilitate workshops that get its people to shape its brand. Others may be more interested in its customers, they may commission market research, or run focus groups themselves. Yet others may be numbers people, experts on data analysis, or on brand valuation, which we explored in Chapter 4. They'll organize all the thinking that emerges during the project, make sense of it, and aim to find new ideas, new insights, and new opportunities.

At the heart of any creative agency are the 'creatives' or designers: the people who make the ads, create the packaging, design the logo, or even specify the whole user experience. Most will have art or design school educations. Many will specialize in the visual side of design; others in the verbal side, and may be known as copywriters. For all these people, the goal is to make the creative leap from idea to form, from rational to emotional, from logical system 2 thinking to intuitive system 1 thinking, so that their client's branding stands out, gets noticed, gets remembered, and changes how people think, feel, and act.

Many agencies now also have a fourth kind of person: technologists. In a world where the main and sometimes only experience of a brand is through a phone or other computer, the technologist has a dual role. They are responsible for helping to create the experiences that people will interact with (using a tap, a swipe, their voice, or a click). And they are responsible for helping colleagues and clients understand how technology continues to change what is possible. They are advocates for the possibilities that technology can bring.

In some agencies, work gets handed from one department to the next, but much more often, people mix together, and everything's done in a way that's as interdisciplinary as possible. Agencies tend to operate in an informal, non-hierarchical way (at least on the surface), but there's always someone in charge. In some agencies, the account manager choreographs everything; in others, creativity matters most, and it's a designer who runs the project; in some (the minority) it's the business thinking (and therefore the strategist) in the lead.

And though most agencies offer a wide range of services, they all have a specific heritage, a home territory. Some, for instance, come from the world of product brands, where packaging was their original skill, and will probably have a sharp commercial focus on product sales. Others may come from the world of corporate and service brands, and their original craft was logo design.

Sometimes these companies are therefore less interested in short-term sales figures, and more in long-term things like identity, ethos, and purpose.

Branding, of course, is a fashion industry. To keep clients interested, to stay relevant, to stimulate new business, to attract the best recruits, to keep themselves on their toes, most agencies frequently change the story they tell, or the proposition they offer. There are exceptions—Siegel+Gale, for instance, consistently talks about 'simplicity'—but many agencies are, paradoxically, better at managing their clients' brands than their own.

Beyond marketing

The big four are essentially marketing services organizations, but branding, as we've seen, these days reaches way beyond marketing. So the global management consultancy firms, like McKinsey or Boston Consulting Group, advise clients on branding too. They've moved beyond their traditionally hard, numbers-led approach into the softer arts of brand-building.

BCG, for example, bought a specialist consultancy called Lighthouse to bolster its ability to advise clients on defining their 'purpose'. And the consulting firm EY, for example, bought the service design agency Seren, because it knows that successful brand-building increasingly depends on the nitty-gritty details of the customer experience.

At the same time, branding consultancies are moving into the world of strategy, and offering clients creative, as opposed to analytic, ways to shape their future success.

New expectations

Branding, then, depends on companies and agencies working effectively together. This happens best when the two sides share an ambition for the project, have a deep understanding of the issues, and trust each other.

But there can be fractures too—particularly when new expectations don't match old assumptions. Recent research suggests that clients now expect to work with agencies in ways that are very different from traditional 20th-century practice.

Branding today is complex, and many companies prefer to break the problem up into chunks, with a specialist agency for each. Traditional agencies, though, want to be in the lead, to be at the top table, to be the 'agency of record', to somehow control the work of other agencies. Instead, they have to get used to being one of many. Google's new brand identity, launched in 2015, was designed in-house, though Google's many agencies may have suggested ideas indirectly. Increasingly, agencies need to think of themselves as contributors, not authors.

Branding, as we've seen, now relies on data as well as creativity. Agencies used to prize creativity above everything; brand managers no longer do. That's one of the reasons that media agencies have become more powerful in recent years. Brand agencies need to get brilliant at quantitative evidence, as well as qualitative imagination.

And branding is no longer just about communication. Consumers believe not what you say, but what you do. What matters, therefore, is the quality of the whole customer experience—and that should now be the primary focus of branding. In a 2015 survey, one brand client said: 'Agencies are largely behind pace. It's now all about putting customers first and designing seamless experiences—driven by tech and innovation.'

Marketing and more

Branding is, in many ways, a curious business. Its origins are the creative worlds of marketing and design, but it has outgrown those worlds, and now deals also in strategy and data. It used to focus on a sales 'proposition', but is now obsessed with a deeper corporate 'purpose'. It's a collision between imagination and commerce, between philosophy and pragmatism, between intuition and evidence, a constant tug between art and science.

People working in branding deal constantly with tensions. Do we try to change the whole company, or focus on marketing first? Do we pursue our internal organizational ambition, or the external customer need? Do we follow our convictions (which encourage us to be bold), or the research (which often pushes us to be conservative)? Do we aim for the long term, or accept that these days it's impossible to predict more than a few weeks ahead? Do we construct a single organizing idea for all our work, or launch many parallel small ideas? These are some of the conundrums that you'll find inside every branding project (Box 5).

Box 5 Muji: no brand

Muji is a global retail brand, but its name literally means 'no brand'. Started in 1980 by the Japanese retailer Seiyu, Muji now has 650 stores globally, selling around £2 billion of housewares and clothing a year. Founded, in its own words, as 'an antithesis to the habits of consumer society at the time', Muji aimed to make simple, useful products from natural materials, to 'maintain an ideal of the proper balance between living and the objects that make it possible'. Though high in concept, Muji is unpretentious in its products, stores, and communication, and its leading light, Ikko Tanaka, was famous for his humility. Muji is a pioneer of a fascinating, paradoxical law of branding: that, for many consumers, the less you behave like a conventionally ostentatious brand, and the more you appear to reject branding itself, the more seductive your brand becomes. Less brand is more brand.

Chapter 6
Branding projects

In February 2014, an Irish marketing expert called Kenny Jacobs joined the low-cost airline Ryanair as the company's first chief marketing officer. In thirty years, Ryanair—with low fares, minimal service, and an aggressive attitude—had become the biggest airline in Europe, carrying eighty million passengers a year. Ryanair didn't do conventional branding—it didn't seem to care about the customer experience, or about its image, or about design—but it had become a huge brand. Ryanair was almost universally known, and almost universally disliked, with a bad press that would have destroyed many other brands (Figure 6).

Jacobs's brief was to change things. With a pledge to listen more to customers, he launched a programme called 'Always Getting Better'. Fares would stay low, but the website and app would become user-friendly, service levels would rise, and Ryanair would fly to more convenient airports at better times of day. The airline would launch a new slogan, promising more than just a price benefit: 'Low fares. Made simple.' Jacobs says that the programme 'galvanised incredibly fast change', generating an impressive 6 per cent increase in Ryanair's 'load factor' (how full its planes are), and that it's been 'the best ride of my life'.

This was a fast, and effective, rebranding project. Jacobs reshaped what Ryanair does, what it says, and (a bit) how it looks, in order

6. Rebranding that worked: Ryanair's project meant big improvements in customer service, summarized by this slogan—and led to a rise in the airline's profitability.

to change the ideas in people's minds. And he did it in a typically Ryanair way. 'We just got on with it,' he reports, 'with no nonsense, and no consultants. We do have a brand strategy, but we don't navel-gaze. I just wrote down the brand on a page and gave it to the CEO.' The rebranding goal was, in a way, modest: 'I have no pretentions to "brand love". We have a functional brand offering a functional product—we're not a high-brand business like Virgin.' And he's more interested in measuring the change in reality than the change in image: 'We track Ryanair the experience, not Ryanair the brand'.

For a high-flying airline, this branding project could not have been more down-to-earth. This is Ryanair's own, authentic way of doing branding. And the best, and longest-lasting, branding is honest. It starts with an internal truth about a product or service or company, and makes that truth external. It nourishes that idea in the minds of consumers. Like all nourishing, this is a continuing daily task, not something that can be done once and for all—so branding keeps refreshing those ideas, and sometimes has to encourage a more profound rethink. For some organizations, branding is a central philosophy, a way of being. For others it's merely one tool among many. But for all, the fake tends to be ephemeral, the authentic lasts.

Just getting on with it

The Ryanair story exemplifies a great deal about current branding practice. Brand managers aim increasingly to listen to customers, and even to involve them in branding projects. Every business, it seems, aspires to be 'customer-centric'. Branding is still driven by the corporation's own agenda, but these priorities are tempered by what customers say they want.

Branding projects today tend to be fast, aiming to produce results in weeks rather than years. Sometimes their aim is highly ambitious—to transform the business, or even to change the world—but often their spirit is more modest and pragmatic. As Jacobs says, 'we just got on with it'. In many industries, the ground feels as if it's constantly shifting, and brand managers therefore have to get something done quickly: there may not be time to achieve perfection in everything. Though a project may be fast, the task of brand-building never ends, so each branding project tends to be just part of a bigger journey.

Branding projects today are rarely linear. There was a time when projects progressed in a logical fashion through a series of stages: first research, then strategy, then design, then implementation. Nowadays, commercial deadlines often demand that items are implemented while the strategy is still being developed. Branding, in any case, is a creative task, and creativity rarely conforms to linear plans. The best work is often done through rapid prototyping—constantly developing, testing, and improving ideas—rather than a traditional stage-by-stage approach.

Twenty years ago, if organizations used outside consultants, they would work in these phases, presenting their work at each step to be signed off by the client. Now, the task is much more interactive, and organizations and their advisors develop ideas in collaboration. Agencies meet their clients at workshops, not at presentations. This is partly because it's the best way to bring the client's first-hand knowledge into the project, and partly because it helps the organization to buy into the emerging ideas. The agency stimulates, provokes, encapsulates, and visualizes thinking, rather than being its author.

Always getting better

Critically, branding projects today focus more on what the organization does than on how it looks or what it says. In this project, Ryanair didn't change its logo or its colours, but its routes, its timetable, and its online booking system. Brands are built through the smallest details of the online and offline experience that customers get. Jacobs measures this constantly and precisely: 'We track Ryanair the experience'.

To make these changes happen, Jacobs created the slogan 'Always Getting Better'. This slogan was aimed not at Ryanair's customers but its employees. Branding projects now almost always start from the inside, because to get the reality of the customer experience to improve, you have to encourage colleagues to change how they do things. Branding projects today aim first to change how employees think, feel, and act.

So branding projects today are increasingly customer-driven, fast, pragmatic, and employee-focused. They're about deeds rather than words, performance rather than philosophy. But they still depend on the power of ideas. Almost all branding projects start by writing something down, some kind of thought that will become the touchstone for everything else. 'I just wrote down the brand on a page,' Jacobs reports. But for all his modesty, this was a very important page for Ryanair: a definition of what the businesses wanted to stand for.

So if this is the overall flavour of branding projects, what do they specifically aim to do? And how do they go about it?

On purpose

Branding, as we've seen, often starts from the inside, and many branding projects aim not to attract customers, but to galvanize the organization's employees. If an organization's performance is slowing, or if its competitors are accelerating, it often uses the disciplines of branding to energize its own people. A re-organization or an acquisition (or a series of acquisitions) may fragment the business, and leave people wondering 'who are we?' A branding project can help create a renewed sense of identity.

Organizations used to talk a lot about their 'vision' (the future state they wanted to work towards) or their 'mission' (their corporate objective), but today, these ideas can seem self-serving. Amazon's vision is to be 'earth's most customer-centric company'. The Japanese earth-moving equipment company Komatsu famously had as its mission 'beat Caterpillar'. But workers today tend to want to make a difference to the wider world, rather than just to win a corporate battle, so purpose statements try to answer the more worthwhile question 'why do we exist?'

This is the most fundamental kind of question, and projects like this usually get kicked off by the CEO—but they're often run by the company's most senior brand experts. Here, branding clearly extends beyond marketing, and indeed projects like this usually invade the territory of strategy: it's hard to be clear about why we exist without also thinking about what we do and where.

Ryanair spent very little time worrying about such philosophical questions, but many organizations believe that a clear answer leads to a whole range of benefits. As well as motivating existing employees, an exciting purpose can attract the best new talent. It can guide and accelerate decision-making across the organization. And for some organizations, it can also attract outside investment.

Most organizations see a value not just in the outcome of a project like this, but also in the process. Often they involve all their senior managers, or even the whole company, in formulating a purpose. This can be complex and time-consuming, but it makes people feel valued, trusted, and influential. And often the 'wisdom of the crowd' is greater than that of the CEO on his or her own.

These projects are tricky. Involving many people can lead to compromise rather than conviction: a watered-down purpose that offends no-one and excites no-one. At the other end, you can end up with a purpose so grand that it's hard to put into practice. The best purpose statements are radical (they want to change the world) but also doable (they're credible and practicable) and useful (they're specific enough to guide day-to-day decisions). The supermarket company Tesco recently changed its purpose from 'to make what matters better together' (preachy and vague) to the much more practical statement 'to serve Britain's shoppers a little better every day'.

What to stand for

Kenny Jacobs wrote the Ryanair brand quickly on a page, but many organizations devote a great deal more time and effort to 'brand strategy'. Branding projects like this aim to define what the product or company wants to stand for in people's minds, and how it's going to make that happen. This is sometimes referred to as 'positioning' the brand.

Often, positioning can be pinned down through two concepts from the world of advertising: proposition and personality. The proposition states what customers get for their money—IKEA's, for example, is 'affordable solutions for better living'. It's the more rational side of branding. The personality, on the other hand, is more emotional: it defines how the product or company should feel to people. When the mobile phone brand Orange was first launched, it described its personality as 'the world through the eyes of a seven-year-old', high on wonder and optimism, with no anxiety or cynicism.

Brand strategy projects are almost always guided by market research, exploring customers, their lives, their needs, and their desires. As Kenny Jacobs says, listening is important. And, increasingly, brand managers see consumers not as one group, or a number of 'segments', but as a set of individuals, whose worldviews can't easily be aggregated—making the task of finding a single proposition much harder.

One or many

Brand strategy projects often explore another complex topic, also beginning with the letter 'p': portfolio. Most large organizations operate with more than one brand. In pursuit of growth, they buy brands, or create new brands to appeal to new markets, and they end up with a portfolio of brands—often complex and hard to manage.

The strategic choices quickly become fascinating. Do we simplify our portfolio, and reduce the number of brands? This option can help focus the organization on high-growth activities. Do we go further and connect our brands together, as Virgin does through the Virgin name? Or do we unify everything under one brand, like IKEA? This can encourage employees to collaborate more, rather than fighting for their own brand. And it can make the marketing operation much more efficient: it's cheaper to build one brand than a hundred. This approach is sometimes called 'branded house': one company with one brand.

But there are also advantages to keeping many brands in play, each looking to customers like an independent business. If one hits problems, the others aren't tainted. And when your customers live in many different cultures, with many different aims in life, you can reach more by spreading your branding bets. This is the 'house of brands' model, exemplified by Procter & Gamble.

Business today is complex, and the desire for simplicity often drives organizations towards the 'branded house' model. But equally, consumers today aren't uniform, and their changing needs are hard to predict: these forces drive businesses towards the 'house of brands'. It's perhaps not surprising that organizations rarely settle for one extreme or the other. Many are on the move, unifying or decentralizing. And others adopt hybrid positions. Coca-Cola, for example, has apparently independent brands like Fanta, plus brands like Dasani that are labelled from Coca-Cola. And its four main products—Coke, Diet Coke, Zero, and Life—look increasingly like flavours of one brand.

As well as sub-brands and product names, some companies deploy special kinds of brands. Ingredient brands convey a special skill or technology. Panasonic, for example, uses 'Lumix' to look good at photography. The BBC has a range of channel brands, from BBC ONE to BBC Radio 4. Many retailers have 'own-label' or 'private label' brands, for products made especially for them. Some use range brands to indicate quality and price, from 'basics' to 'best'. Others invent seemingly independent brands that are carefully designed to look a bit like the big familiar brands, or even like small craft brands, with names like 'Ocean Sea' or 'Rowan Hill Bakery'. The discounters Aldi and Lidl are famous for this.

The brand team also looks at architecture outside the company—what other brands do we want to be associated with? Companies use 'endorsements' to add value to their brands—for example, some L'Oréal products are endorsed by the singer Cheryl Cole. They use sponsorship to reach new customers: the airline Emirates became famous to British consumers by sponsoring Arsenal. They use alliances to extend their reach. Thai Airways, by joining Star Alliance, can offer more routes and more lounges. And they get into new markets by starting joint ventures, often with competitors: Aviva entered the life insurance market in Turkey by teaming up with local insurer Sabanci to form AvivaSA.

Getting the product right

These branding projects—defining purpose, proposition, personality, or portfolio—largely produce words, strategies, plans. But as we've seen, the emphasis is increasingly on deeds. Projects like Ryanair's start with the 'offer'—the product or service that customers get. This is the best way to generate rapid increases in revenue or profitability. Jeff Bezos, founder of Amazon, says, 'In the old world, you devoted 30% of your time to building a great service and 70% of your time to shouting about it. In the new world, that inverts.'

There's always a trade-off here between improving what exists, and introducing something new. Often the quickest way to improve your brand—to upgrade the ideas in consumers' minds—is to find out what they most dislike about your current offering, and fix those problems. This was where Ryanair started—by switching to airports nearer to city centres, and by making the online purchase process much less arduous.

Brand managers also look at pricing and distribution. Pushing the price down can make your product more accessible and get your brand into the minds of many more people. But pushing the price up can increase people's sense of its quality, and paradoxically make it more valuable. Adjusting the pricing strategy—without actually changing the product at all—can make a big impact on the brand in people's minds. And distribution has a similar effect: do you want to be seen as universally available, and perhaps a daily purchase? Or as rare and special—something you have to make an effort to track down and buy?

But most brand managers are also keen to innovate—not least to keep their brand fresh in people's minds. Some adopt a method known as 'brand-driven innovation'. They use the idea that they want to stand for to inspire new product ideas, and to filter out ideas that won't build the brand. Virgin, for instance, wants its brand to stand for 'convention-breaking', so when Virgin Atlantic designed a new Upper Class cabin, its people asked themselves 'What ingrained conventions can we break to serve the user better?' And it's now common to involve customers in 'co-creating' new products—LEGO's Mindstorms, kits from which people can make programmable robots, are an example of a successful user-generated new product.

In your experience

The most fashionable phrase is branding now is probably 'experience design'. The idea is to go deeper than just fixing problems with the product, or adjusting pricing or distribution, and deeper even than introducing new products. Instead, brand managers aim to connect together everything the customer experiences, into one seamless journey. For almost every business, this now means unifying what happens online with what happens offline—not an easy task. By giving the customer an experience that's both seamless and distinctive, this kind of project creates a much deeper impression of the brand in people's minds, and ideally leads to a deeper and longer relationship between company and consumer.

Branding projects like these often apply techniques originally created to design online user interfaces. They define 'personas'—imaginary people who typify particular kinds of customer—and the design work is done through the eyes of these personas. They map the 'customer journeys' these personas take, from first encountering the product or company, through to using it and recommending it to others. And they define 'experience principles' that guide the second-by-second design decisions that they make.

An experience is, of course, something that plays out over time, so it's natural to design customer experiences through the metaphor of the journey, or even the story. To build its brand, Airbnb specified its ideal customer experience, step by step, in the form of a Disney-style film storyboard.

The death of advertising?

Improving the product, or the whole customer experience, is where branding projects often start. But the world needs to know about the great new offer, so marketing communications—the original home of branding—are still critically important.

To influence their image or presence, to get their message into the world, organizations deploy the whole range of media. The most obvious, of course, is advertising, in all its forms: the traditional home of brand-building. Though print advertising is in steep decline, online has become the front-line in advertising, where complex techniques are deployed like programmatic advertising (in which software, rather than people, buy the advertising space). And the familiar television commercial is still an immensely powerful way to associate ideas and emotions with a product.

Advertising is sometimes referred to as 'paid media', and it's the most expensive form of communication. The cheapest kind is what's called 'owned media'—your website, your shop displays, your presentations, where everything is entirely under your control. Then there's 'earned media'—coverage in blogs, social media, television, and the press. This is almost impossible to control, but when it works in your favour, it's probably the most effective form of communication—because increasingly consumers believe not what you say, but what others say about you.

In fact, because people are getting so good at decoding, and discounting, traditional sales messages, many companies are investing heavily in 'content marketing'. Instead of sales talk, they create and share useful content on the things that matter to consumers. Pampers, for instance, has become a source of guidance on childcare. Wherever possible, they aim to make material that people want to share with each other through social media, because people respond much more warmly to things they hear from each other than to things they hear from companies. Indeed, Red Bull now seems to put as much effort into making content as it does into making soft drinks. For years, Benetton built its brand through provocative reportage in its magazine *Colors*. The camera company GoPro has built its brand through films on YouTube, not conventional advertising. Others create branded spaces as a way to tell a subtler story than advertising can—like the Vans skate parks in California and London, or the Tesla and Dyson stores in London's Oxford Street.

This is all currently controversial. Some say that content marketing is the right strategy, particularly as a way to deepen relationships with existing consumers. Others say this is a wasted investment: in a world of disloyal, promiscuous customers, you have to keep attracting new consumers to replace those who leave you, and the best way to do that is still traditional advertising. Brand expert Byron Sharp, with a great deal of data as evidence, argues that you need to get noticed by new customers, not to become friends with old ones.

Behind the scenes, another kind of communication is vital in branding. 'Stakeholder management' is the task of keeping the most influential individuals on your side—politicians, policy-makers, and regulators. The health of an oil business like Shell, for instance, may depend much more on the brand in these people's minds than it does on consumers' perceptions.

The culture is the brand

We've looked at many kinds of branding project, from purpose to experience, from portfolio strategy to content marketing. But they all depend on people—on mobilizing the organization's employees to get with the brand.

Many branding projects therefore aim to create the right climate inside the organization—or, to put it another way, to change its culture. Particularly in service businesses, customers' impressions of the brand depend on their experience of the brand's people. Most organizations now realize that, though a brand is an external phenomenon, out there in the minds of customers, branding starts with the internal. You need your own people to understand what you want to stand for, to believe in it, to have all the right skills, and to use your brand identity well, in order to do the right things for customers. Indeed, Tony Hseih, who runs the online shoe retailer Zappos, says 'your culture is your brand'.

So, to help nurture the right company culture, organizations invest in ambitious 'employee engagement' programmes, in order to get as many people as possible to 'live the brand'. And the brand thinking can become a corporate mantra. In companies like John Lewis, Nordstrom, Huawei, and Netflix, the brand idea becomes a very useful leadership tool, guiding people's decisions and raising their standards without telling them exactly what to do. It moves beyond the traditional 'command and control' style of management, exerting a subtler power. A Google employee said to me: 'The brand goes before us, and therefore people expect us to be impressive, so that certainly makes us all raise our game'.

Organizations often appoint influential employees to be 'brand ambassadors', or even 'brand evangelists', spreading the branding message to colleagues and the outside world. The label is interesting—in some cultures, diplomacy is the right metaphor, in others, religion. The eventual aim is to have every employee as a brand advocate, and to eliminate the 'brand saboteurs' that you'll find lurking inside many organizations.

But it's not enough to have a high-energy culture: to deliver its product brilliantly, an organization also needs the right skills. Less glamorous than 'culture', but even more important, is 'capability'. To achieve its mantra of 'always getting better', a business like Ryanair must invest in recruitment, training, and technology.

Since 1961, McDonald's has inculcated over 80,000 restaurant managers in essential skills through its 'Hamburger University' in Chicago. In 2001, Toyota codified its fourteen-step methodology as the Toyota Way. Companies like Vodafone use online systems to spread learning rapidly—often with employees teaching each other how best to do things, by making short videos. More strategically, many organizations realize they can't create the right brand on their own, and bring in the skills they need through partnerships and alliances. Virgin, for example, has largely built its brand through joint ventures with specialists: with Singapore Airlines (and, more recently, Delta) for Virgin Atlantic, with Stagecoach for Virgin Trains, and so on.

The magic of design

Some branding projects are purely about design—changing the way the organizations looks and talks is still a powerful way to change how people think, feel, and act.

But design has a role to play in every kind of branding project. Design turns the logical into the intuitive, and at its best turns prose into poetry. Design can therefore humanize a purpose statement. It brings a proposition and personality off the page and into the world. It makes visual sense of a portfolio. It activates an offer, and fleshes out an experience.

This is where logical thought becomes unexpected, informal, personal, rule-breaking, or provocative. Branding can deploy irony: *LazyTown*, for example, is an Icelandic television show that encourages children to be active. It can even be incomprehensible. Most consumers don't know what the Audi slogan *Vorsprung durch Technik* means, but it still vividly conveys a powerful Germanic mystique. Through tricks like this, the reasonable becomes unreasonable. In the language of the neuroscientists, design by-passes rational thinking and directly triggers people's intuitive, or system 1, responses.

Traditionally, brand designers have concentrated on the visual elements—the most obvious signifiers—of the brand, such as its logo, colours, and typefaces. But these are just part of a much larger system. As well as the visual dimension, designers now give a great deal of attention to the verbal. This includes the brand name, product naming systems and slogans, but also the brand's 'tone of voice', or the style in which everything is written. Businesses like Innocent Drinks have a particularly distinctive writing style, and many others are now trying to achieve the same impact. Carlsberg can be recognized just by one word, 'probably'.

Designers also work carefully on the sensory dimensions of the brand. Smells, tastes, gestures, and textures can be very effective triggers of system 1 reactions. The hotel group Kempinski sprays its lobbies with a distinctive smell. Car-makers design the precise 'clunk' sound their car doors make when being closed. And the Spanish hotel group Meliá even encourages its staff to put their right hand on their hearts when greeting a customer—a distinctive brand gesture.

But for many companies, there's an even more important dimension of brand design: the interactive. Designers carefully consider the pixel-by-pixel, second-by-second details of the online user interface—because that's the most effective way of nurturing in customers' minds the right kind of impressions of the brand. WeChat, the Chinese messaging app, is a master of user interface design.

Some designers talk about 'touchpoints'—all the different things that a customer (or employee or investor) sees or touches, and that influence their sense of what the brand is all about. But this could be a static and fragmented way of thinking—designing many separate touchpoints—and it's now common, as we've seen, for designers to look at the whole customer experience, often as a 'customer journey' through time.

As with any creative activity, tastes, judgements, and conventions change over time. Brands take their cues from each other, just as artists influence other artists. The fashion at the moment is for purism, for stripping things back to essentials. Brand visual identities have often used shadows, highlights, and textures to give an illusion of three dimensions. Now the fashion—from Apple to Coca-Cola—is for simple 'flat' graphics. And brand naming has moved from made-up words (Google, Skype, Spotify) to simple real words (Uber, Vine, Slack).

Honestly useful

Design, in its many dimensions, is a critical tool in every successful branding project. In some projects, it's about creating an unmissable logo. In others, it may mean defining exactly what happens when a user clicks on 'Checkout', or writing a simple mantra like 'Always Getting Better'. The emphasis now is less on design as styling, much more on design as problem-solving—and that's because people believe the reality they experience. Branding is less about myth-making, more about good, honest usefulness (Box 6).

Box 6 Superdry: English Japanese

Superdry is a global clothing retailer that has shot to success in the last ten years, famous for the striking Japanese lettering on its products. But Superdry comes not from Tokyo but from Cheltenham, England. The brand was founded in 1985 by Julian Dunkerton as Cult Clothing, with Superdry as an in-house brand. But Superdry turned out to be the more potent brand and, by 2012, all the Cult stores had changed their name to Superdry. Now there are over 500 stores in almost fifty countries. The company focuses, it says, on high-quality products that fuse vintage Americana and Japanese-inspired graphics, with a British style. The Japanese lettering is largely nonsense and random, but as a branding device it works brilliantly—except, apparently, in Japan.

Chapter 7
The ethics of branding

In 1988, a Dutch development agency called Solidaridad created a set of 'fair trade' standards that would guarantee a decent living for producers. Solidaridad's idea was to use branding to encourage consumers in rich countries to change their buying behaviour: to pay more for ethical products.

The idea rapidly spread beyond the Netherlands. A Fairtrade Labelling Organisation was set up, and in 2002 it launched a new brand, Fairtrade (Figure 7). Producers join a local cooperative and they benefit from advice and training, as well as a guaranteed minimum price.

The scheme is not perfect. Fairtrade products command a high price, and critics say that too much of this premium is kept by the retailers. And the system puts non-Fairtrade farmers at a serious disadvantage. Nevertheless, by 2013, consumers could choose from 30,000 different Fairtrade products, and they spent 5.5 billion euros buying them. The branding project had worked. And the scheme was helping 1.2 million workers and farmers in seventy-four countries.

Branding, clearly, is a powerful force. But is it always a force for good? There are reasons to be optimistic. Increasingly,

7. Social change: the Fairtrade brand encourages people to choose products that benefit their producers, rather than exploiting them.

commercial profit depends on social purpose, and branding has to be good in order to make money.

Stories or lies?

Take another supermarket product. If you go shopping for salmon in Marks & Spencer in Britain, you'll find packages that say (for example) 'Lochmuir Salmon en croute'. It sounds delicious. Most people in Britain know that 'loch' is a Scottish lake, so it's easy to imagine that this salmon comes from a beautiful lake somewhere in the highlands. But if you go to Google Maps, and search for 'Lochmuir', you get an error message: 'We could not find Lochmuir. Make sure your search is spelled correctly.' Why is this? Because there's no such place—it's an invention of the branding people, to create a sense of provenance, and so to add value to the product.

Similarly, you might expect that Superdry comes from Japan—but, as we've just seen, it was founded in Cheltenham, England, in 1985. You might think that Häagen-Dazs is Scandinavian, but it's from New York. You might imagine that Crabtree and Evelyn is an old English company that goes back centuries, but it was set up by an American and two British people in Massachusetts in 1972. So when does colourful storytelling turn into misleading the consumer? Given that branding is designed to change how we think, feel, and act, when does its influence become pernicious?

There have been many critics of brands and branding over the years. The American journalist Vance Packard wrote an engrossing book called *The Hidden Persuaders*, back in 1957. He exposes the then-fashionable practice of motivational research, in which advertising people tapped into people's subconcious psychological processes to sell things (even using tricks, now banned, like subliminal advertising). 'Many of us', he concludes, 'are being influenced and manipulated, far more than we realize, in the patterns of our everyday lives.' So branding, and some of the practices it involves, can involve systematically tricking or manipulating people.

The British art critic John Berger made a television series in 1972 called *Ways of Seeing*, which became a book too. It's a brilliant Marxist analysis of the meanings, motives, and economics behind the images we see in art, and one programme analyses what Berger calls 'publicity', by which he means advertising and its related practices—an art that we might today call 'branding'. Berger concludes that 'the purpose of publicity is to make the spectator marginally dissatisfied with his present way of life'. Branding deliberately makes people unhappy with what they have, in order to induce them to buy more. It's the systematic creation of low-grade misery.

Most famously of all, the Canadian journalist Naomi Klein wrote a world best-seller in 2000, *No Logo*. This is an exploration of the way brands have invaded every area of life, including schools, and of the dubious practices of the big brand-owners, such as the use of sweatshops in developing countries to make a lot of the world's branded clothing. Klein predicts that 'as more young people discover the brand-name secrets of the global logo web, their outrage will fuel the next big political movement'. Her prediction hasn't entirely come true, but she has sparked an unprecedented level of public scrutiny of the branded multinationals.

These books attack something bigger than branding: the overweening practices of the big multinational corporations, or the entire economic system of capitalism. They all appeal to the teenager in us, the rebel, the conspiracy-theorist. Yet they do also hit hard at the trickery and sometimes hypocrisy of branding—and at the way that branding is not just a series of one-off deceptions but a system, a climate that we can't easily escape from.

But is this the only way to see branding? Clearly not.

The gaiety of nations

Branding also has many positive effects. For consumers, it creates variety and guides choice. To keep their brands fresh in our minds, companies constantly develop new products and services. And without branding, it would be hard to identify and find the things we're looking for. If we want to quench our thirst, or paint our house, or get a loan, or watch a television show, branding guides us, helps us get what we want. Imagine a brand-free supermarket, with just one product in every category.

Brands make the world more predictable, and so reduce the anxiety of day-to-day life. Without brands, we wouldn't know what level of quality to expect from a product. We wouldn't know who or what to trust. Late at night, in a strange city, it can be very reassuring to find a McDonald's. Being a consumer is a worrying job, with a constant risk of making bad buying decisions, and one of the main psychological benefits of branding is to reduce that anxiety.

Branding also raises aspirations, and helps make good things more accessible: you could argue that it's a democratizing force. Penguin Books was founded in the 1930s to make good reading affordable to the new middle classes, and its founder, Allen Lane, spoke of it as not just a publisher but also a brand. It's partly the brand power of something like Tate in London or MoMA in New York that brings things like contemporary art to more people. You could also argue that it's through the anxiety-reducing power of branding that people try out new products and experiences. Tesco's former CEO, Terry Leahy, has argued that 'the British working class moved upmarket with us', and that the Tesco brand encouraged people to try a whole range of exotic new foods. The reassurance of airline and hotel brands, for example, encourages us to try new countries and new cultures.

Brands can make people feel better about themselves. Rightly or wrongly, they make us feel we've made the smart choice, or that we're the kind of people we've always wanted to be. Branding gives products and services extra meaning, extra value—they help us to show off to others, or just to quietly feel better about ourselves. They may give us a sense of identity and belonging, like LEGO's brand communities, and they get us to participate in the process of creating meaning. And some branding gives us a power we wouldn't otherwise have had. It's through the power of brands like eBay and Etsy that we're able to sell things to the world.

Held to account

Branding can be good not just for consumers, but also for workers. Working for a good brand makes work feel more worthwhile. Employees feel a stronger sense of belonging, and that their work is worth doing, for a business with a strong brand like Nordstrom or John Lewis. And a clear statement of what you want to stand for makes for better decision-making. A brand can give workers guidance on what to do and how to do it—like Tesco's mantra 'to serve Britain's shoppers a little better every day', or the Indian conglomerate Mahindra's idea of enabling people 'to rise'.

Branding, clearly, is good for the economy. Because the primary role of branding is to stimulate buying (and repeated buying), it clearly helps create sales; and you could argue that the world's economic growth over the last century has been at least partly driven by the power of brands. The gross world product in 1920 was less than $2 trillion, now it's well over $50 trillion (at 1990 prices)—could that have happened without branding?

For society, branding improves quality, and makes corporations accountable. Because brands are a guarantee of a certain level of quality, they tend to improve quality overall. And because a brand is so valuable to its owner, it's motivated to fix anything that could damage the brand—which is why, for example, Primark moved so rapidly in 2013 to improve conditions in its factories in

Bangladesh. Brands in fact become a focus for scrutiny by ethical consumers—a scrutiny that would be much harder in an unbranded world.

At a less serious level, brands add to the gaiety of nations. Imagine how drab a brand-less world would be—and how humourless, if it didn't allow the Japanese fantasy of Superdry or the imaginary heritage of Crabtree & Evelyn. These stories add value for the consumer. And brands bring people closer together. Apple, Samsung, Facebook, Twitter, Nike, Adidas are today's lingua franca: a lexicon of meanings that we all share.

Endless dissatisfaction

But there's a negative side to almost all these arguments. For consumers, branding can create homogeneity and reduce choice. Although at one level we've never had more goods and services to choose from, at another level there's less choice. The big global brand corporations drive out local, unbranded businesses, so that every city in the world now offers exactly the same range of shops, hotels, and even restaurants: Zara, Holiday Inn, Hard Rock Café. And in the online world, where brands help generate network effects, the result tends to be quasi-monopoly—Google, Wikipedia, eBay, Instagram.

Brands can create a false sense of security. In one way they guarantee quality, but they also encourage us to stop thinking—to assume, for example, that every ingredient in branded food must be healthy.

They trick people into buying things they don't need. You could say that this is the essence of branding: to create desire. Branding gets people to pay more than they need to; to buy and consume things they don't need; and to buy things that are bad for them, from cigarettes to sugary drinks. For some they become an addiction, they become label addicts.

Brands can make people feel dissatisfied with their lives, as John Berger has argued. Because branding creates desire, it doesn't create satisfaction or happiness. Like some addictive drugs, it stimulates the production of dopamine in the brain, making us constantly want more—the next version of the iPhone, the next BMW model up. Branding—it could be argued—creates permanently unsatisfied desires, rather like Oscar Wilde's description of the cigarette: 'A cigarette is the perfect pleasure; it is exquisite and leaves one unsatisfied'.

Commercializing everything

You could argue that branding tricks employees into serving shareholders' interests, not their own. Today's employees, many serving carefully branded organizations, work hours that would have looked shocking in Victorian times, answering emails from breakfast to bedtime (and after). The glamour of the brand they work for, you could argue, leads them to put in far more labour than they're actually paid for.

For the economy, just as branding stimulates economic growth, it also fuels unsustainable levels of consumption, and therefore unsustainable levels of production. It creates a cycle in which resources are depleted, oceans are polluted, habitats are destroyed, and climate patterns are changed.

And for society, brands can be a mask behind which organizations can do wrong. Big, familiar, respected brands can make society assume that everything behind the scenes is OK, as the world saw in 2015 when Volkswagen's systematic deceptions about emission levels were revealed.

Branding may add colour, but it also commercializes everything, and makes everything banal. It helps turn religious festivals into commercial bonanzas. It brings commerce into schools, universities, museums, and galleries. In the interests of simplicity, brand managers can reduce a living, changing multi-dimensional entity like a city into a crass slogan: Edinburgh, for instance, becomes 'inspiring capital'.

And though brands unite us, they also divide the haves from the have-nots. They make it very visible who can afford an iPhone, and who has to make do with an ancient Nokia.

Branding for social change

So what conclusion can we come to? The negatives are true, and I wouldn't want to minimize them, or encourage complacency. But the most effective branding is ethical, in the sense that it's the projection of a truth: branding that lies tends not to last.

And, overall, the effect of branding is to force things into the open. By operating under brand names, by using these powerful signs, companies are highly visible. They're important in people's lives, and therefore a natural object of scrutiny. People tend to be aware of branding and how it works, even while obeying its iron law. The rise of internet culture has amplified people's knowledge of brands and their power to investigate them—as well as fuelling non-deferential, anti-institutional attitudes. Through social media, individuals have gained the power to call companies to account, and in recent years consumers have boycotted companies like Amazon, Burberry, and Chevron. These boycotts may not destroy the brand, but they often do instigate changes in corporate policy. So for big companies, there's nowhere to hide.

And if branding changes how people think, feel, and act, can it also do that to achieve social change? Could branding help people and the planet? Clearly, branding can encourage short-term behaviour that leads to increased wellbeing. Fairtrade is an example. Unilever brands its Lifebuoy soap for its hygienic qualities, and runs a health education programme in rural India that it claims has reached seventy million people.

Branding can also create long-term habits that lead to increased sustainability. Zipcar, for example, encourages people to share cars rather than owning them, and claims that every Zipcar takes seventeen privately owned cars off the road. BlaBlaCar and Liftshare aim for similar effects, through ride-sharing. Method makes environmentally friendly cleaning products attractive to buy. Wikipedia is a brand that has encouraged thousands of contributors to add, through voluntary work, to the world's intellectual resources (Box 7).

Girl Effect is an organization—originally set up by Nike—that aims to use the power of media brands to change the attitudes and behaviours of teenage girls, particularly in the developing world, guiding them towards better health and education. Its first two brands, Yegna in Ethiopia and Ni-Nyampinga in Rwanda, offer radio programmes, girl bands, magazines, and websites that show teenage girls new social norms. The branding draws millions in

Box 7 Wikipedia: a labour of love

Wikipedia is a global brand run not by expert employees, but by volunteers. Founded in 2001 by Jimmy Wales, and launched in 2001, its mission is 'to compile the sum of all human knowledge'. Wikipedia now contains forty million articles in 250 different languages. Though it's crowdsourced, rather than written by scholars, it's generally highly reliable, and studies have shown that Wikipedia is often just as accurate as *Encyclopedia Britannica*, the institution that it has, in many ways, replaced. The English Wikipedia now has around 120,000 active editors. What gets people to build a global encyclopedia, and a global brand, for nothing? It's called the 'incentive economy'—prestige, recognition, a desire for fact, an obsession with accuracy. But also—and this is the power of many newer brands—just the feeling of taking part in, of being part of, something worthwhile.

and transforms what is seen as 'normal'. The brands then take on a life of their own, as audiences start to identify themselves as, for instance, 'Yegna girls', and start to feel a much stronger sense of self-confidence.

Good business

Perhaps the strongest reason for a positive view of branding is the increasing interdependency between commercial and social impact. After a string of corporate scandals and crashes—Enron, BP, Lehman Brothers, Volkswagen—people demand a much higher level of social responsibility. To earn, and keep, the commitment of the people who matter—consumers, employees, regulators, the media—organizations now keenly pursue social as well as commercial impact. Companies like Unilever also see social objectives as a way to inspire innovation, and to become much more efficient in the use of scarce resources. Walmart, the world's largest retailer, sees sustainability as good business, and social responsibility helps it to live up to its brand slogan 'Save Money. Live Better'. Profit, for most of the world's CEOs, now depends partly on purpose. Increasingly, therefore, organizations will have to use their brands not just to achieve commercial aims, but to secure social goals too.

Chapter 8
A future for branding?

We've seen that branding, though a very old practice, has recently become a big topic, a board-room priority, and a field of academic research. Its scope has expanded into culture, politics, education, cities, countries, celebrities, and more. But how is the practice of branding changing? Has it reached its peak? Or does it have a long future ahead of it?

It's possible to discern three areas in which change is happening: the scope of branding (what gets branded), the target of branding (who branding is for), and the spirit of branding (how branding works). In each of these, there's no simple transition from the old to the new. Instead, there's a dialectic, a conflict between two forces. It's rather like a soap opera, with three strong storylines. Like all good storylines, they thrive on conflict: in each case, there's not a clear winner, only opposing forces. But if there's one thought that unites these storylines, it's that traditional branding is now challenged by a newer, less corporate alternative.

What gets branded?

There's a live debate in business about the best way to organize, or the best form of organization—and therefore what kind of organizational entity needs to be branded.

The publicly owned corporation continues to be the dominant form. This kind of organization, answerable to its shareholders, and seeking constant growth in profits, proved itself in the last century to be a highly effective way of making money. Apple is, perhaps, the supreme example: an astonishingly wealthy empire sitting on cash reserves of $200 billion. In a globalized world, scale is more important than ever, so businesses continue to merge together into ever greater units: recently Kraft, for instance, has joined Heinz, and Shell has merged with BG. These corporations aim to be self-sufficient, to do things themselves, to own their intellectual property. In the business landscape, they are corporate citadels.

But at the same time, many alternative organizational forms have grown in strength. Some of the world's biggest companies today are state-owned (like China Mobile) or privately owned (like IKEA). In some markets, employee-owned co-operatives (John Lewis, Mondragon) are very successful. Even China's Huawei is partly employee-owned. There's a new breed of social enterprises, like Cafédirect, or benefit corporations, like Etsy, Patagonia, and the British food company COOK. There are much looser, but clearly branded, movements—more 'organizings' than 'organizations'—like the Black Lives Matter movement. And the last ten years have seen, of course, an unprecedented crop of start-ups. None of these organizations is driven by the short-term demands of the stockmarket; some of them are fuelled by an anti-corporate spirit; almost all of them aim for goals beyond pure profit.

The traditional corporation uses branding as a way to maximize shareholder value, by achieving price premiums and securing long-term revenues. But alternative forms of organization may have other aims too. Social enterprises may want to build support for a particular cause; start-ups in the digital world may be aiming not for immediate revenue but for network effects.

And many organizations—both conventional and alternative in form—are operating in a much more collaborative way. For example, when business depends on complex technologies that are hugely expensive to develop, they choose to work with organizations that have those technologies, rather than developing them for themselves. This means organizations are acting less as self-sufficient citadels, and much more in constellations with others. This can feel very different. Phil Mirvis, an academic expert on organizations, says 'the company is no longer the centre of its universe'. Instead of standing at centre-stage, controlling a web of suppliers and distributors, companies find themselves working as equal partners with collaborators (and, often, competitors) in a kind of organizational ecosystem.

Citadel or constellation

The storyline here, then, is the clash between two philosophies: the citadel and the constellation. You could see Apple as the model citadel, and Google as a conspicuous constellation. And yet of course the truth is more complex. Apple's App Store depends on a constellation of independent developers, and Google's parent Alphabet is turning into a conventional-looking conglomerate. Organizations that begin as rebellious start-ups grow, and inevitably take on the apparatus of the traditional corporation.

In branding, the consequences are fascinating. Traditional global brands, sometimes called 'powerbrands', continue to grow: Apple, Pepsi, Mercedes-Benz, Vodafone, and many more. Some of them, though, occasionally try to look small and un-corporate, using a trick known as 'debranding'. Starbucks, for instance, has a neighbourhood coffee shop in Seattle called Roy Street Coffee and Tea. Its website says it's 'inspired by Starbucks', but actually it's owned by Starbucks.

At the same time, paradoxically, many of the world's newer brands have tried to look *more* corporate. Many online businesses started life with informal, unsophisticated, almost hand-made, brand identities. The priority for them was a brilliant product and a memorable name, not a slick logo. Some, like Instagram and Airbnb, were handwritten. Others, such as Yahoo and eBay, were bouncy and cartoon-like. Even the mighty Google had a typographically awkward logo. One by one, they have switched to much more carefully designed, much more conventional, much more corporate brand identities, in order to signal to users and regulators that they are proper, grown-up, money-making businesses.

Behind the scenes, ownership is changing—for example, Zipcar has been bought by Avis and Yahoo by Verizon—and it remains to be seen how these version 5 brands will develop under new owners. Some internet brand companies are now partnering with traditional businesses: Alphabet, for instance, has set up a bioelectronics business with GlaxoSmithKline, called Galvani. How will these joint ventures get branded?

At the same time, big brands have emerged that are shared by many companies. Perhaps the biggest brand on the planet is Android, which, though legally owned by Google, is in practice shared among hundreds of phone and tablet makers.

Brand as affiliation

The new model that's emerging is the purposeful constellation—organizations joining together to pursue more than just commercial goals. With social media, memes and hashtags can become global phenomena in a matter of hours. They are symbols that people adopt, identify with, give meaning to, and share. Though they're owned by no-one, and certainly not by any commercial organization, they are brands. In the wake of the terrorist attack in 2015 on the French satirical newspaper *Charlie Hebdo*, millions of people used the slogan 'Je suis Charlie'. The phrase became a mark of affiliation, a temporary but potent un-corporate brand.

So, though branding is still usually about positioning and ownership, it's increasingly also about purpose and *affiliation*. Its dominant role is still to get people to buy things, but there's an emerging role: to give people, and other organizations, a reason to affiliate. The conference organizer TED—whose purpose is to spread 'ideas worth sharing'—has given up a degree of control over its brand, allowing groups around the world to affiliate to the brand and organize their own TEDx events.

These shifts in the nature of the organization will continue, and we'll see more branding that aims to be un-corporate in one way or another: to signal social purpose, to look small and local, to bring organizations together, and to exert charm rather than just power.

Of course, if a brand is an intrinsically corporate thing and the world is moving towards the un-corporate, there will no longer be a place for it. Perhaps, in an un-corporate world, there will just be shifting, informal 'organizings', none of which is permanent enough to build a brand.

Who's branding for?

While organizations are morphing in form, another battle is playing out: a power struggle between the producer of goods (the company) and consumer (the people). When it comes to branding, who is in the driving seat?

Over the last ten years or so, producers have grown hugely in power, particularly through the data they have about consumers. Because we now consume so much online, we all leave a trail of data, revealing precisely where we are, what we buy, what we read and watch, and how our preferences are changing over time. This data is, of course, invaluable to producers, and selling the data is now a widespread (though largely invisible) economic activity. Indeed, it's the value of this data that pays for many of those online services that appear to be free. As the chilling phrase goes, 'If it's free, you're the product'.

But at the same time, the internet has given the consumer unprecedented powers. Consumers can now compare products instantly, get impartial products reviews from thousands of their peers, and make very public complaints through social media—all of which was impossible only a few years ago. Alternatively, they can become a 'collaborative consumer', rejecting the old mode of consumption in which each of us owns our own property, in favour of a new mode where goods are shared among many. There's currently, for example, a discernible shift away from car ownership among younger people, towards car clubs like Zipcar—a worrying trend for car manufacturers who could face massively declining sales.

And it's never been easier for consumers to fund, make, or sell things themselves, cutting out the traditional producer entirely. Kickstarter, for instance, makes us all venture capitalists; eBay makes everyone a retailer; Airbnb means anyone can be a mini-hotelier; and with Uber you start your own taxi business. Alongside all this is a massive growth in small-scale production: the 'maker movement' includes the rise of craftspeople using sites like Etsy; and 'hacker culture' is the emerging subculture of clever people finding new ways to solve problems, often using software coding (to be distinguished from the darker kind of hackers who break into computer systems).

The *consommacteur*

Many of these phenomena are, of course, minority activities, but the underlying shift in mindset is undoubtedly mainstream. Research suggests that, back in 2006, 90 per cent of internet users were passive, simply consuming information. Just six years later, the ratio had switched, and 87 per cent of users were actively contributing content—even if only posting their most recent selfie on Facebook. The internet has activated the consumer, and what the French call the *consommacteur*—half consumer, half actor—is now mainstream.

In some ways, technology has made the consumer more individualistic, more atomized, and everyone has become a one-person brand. In others, it has made it much easier to coalesce into groups, networks, communities, or what are fashionably called 'tribes'.

Academics have taken this thinking further, and proposed an idea called 'service-dominant logic', which questions the traditional sharp distinction between producer and consumer. It proposes that, when consumers buy a service, they almost always play an active role in the production of value. By using the service, they co-create its value. Indeed, they determine what, for them, constitutes value. When I use an airline like Lufthansa, I do some of the work: printing my boarding card, carrying my cabin bag, and so on. When I post a review on Tripadvisor, I'm helping make Tripadvisor a more valuable service.

And the theory goes further and suggests that all exchanges, of products as well as services, are like this—that it's actually better to think of products as a kind of service, which is why the logic is 'service-dominant'. The enterprise, it's argued, cannot actually deliver value. Its power is limited to offering 'value propositions', which the consumer transforms into value. A Hyundai car, a Forever 21 top, even an Oreo biscuit, has no value until someone uses it.

Back in the marketplace, there's an interesting battle, with branding as an important weapon. Producers, with ever greater data in their hands, are getting better at pushing products out, using branding to build loyalty, and deploying a battery of techniques to sell us things at precisely the moment we're most likely to buy. Consumers, at the same time, are becoming cannier, more suspicious, much less loyal, and readier to reject traditional consumption. And both phenomena happen at the same time. Most of us are resistant to branding at one moment, and yet seduced by it at the next.

It's now common practice for companies to recognize a shift in power, and to say that their brands are now 'owned' by or 'co-created' by their customers. At a minimum, this means that organizations recognize that their brands exist outside themselves, in the minds of people out in the world, and can't therefore be directly controlled. All you can do is to nudge your customers towards creating the 'right' kind of meaning. As Marty Neumeier says in his book *The Brand Flip*: 'A brand is not owned by the company, but by the customers who draw meaning from it. Your brand isn't what *you* say it is. It's what *they* say it is.' Pushing this thought to its conclusion, many brand managers now conceive their brands from the outside in, and enlist customers as their most important brand-builders.

Brand as platform

Out of the battle has emerged the idea of the *platform*. Received wisdom now in Silicon Valley is that companies should make not products to sell to consumers, but platforms on which people can do things: platforms like eBay, or the App Store, or Uber. Marketing people talk less about building emotional 'loyalty', and more about making things that are simply 'useful' to people. The brand expert John Willshire neatly contrasts traditional branding, which he describes as 'making people want things', with the newer mode, 'making things people want'. Out go the advertising people who aim to create desire; in come product and experience designers who just want to make something useful. Branding is more functional, and brand identities more utilitarian. There's a new (and probably often false) modesty in the air.

The question then about these platform brands is: whose are they anyway? Created by a 'producer' company, like eBay, they become the tool of the 'consumer': they become the means by which users achieve their goals. An eBay seller relies on the probity of the eBay brand. The Uber and Airbnb brands are essential badges for Uber drivers and Airbnb hosts. Indeed, Airbnb recognized this

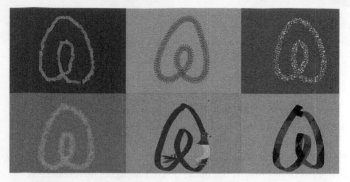

8. A shared brand: the Airbnb logo is called 'bélo', and it's designed for Airbnb hosts to adopt and adapt, making it their own.

in 2014 by redesigning its logo—called 'bélo'—as a kind of template that its hosts can adopt, adapt, and redraw (Figure 8). By 2016, 160,000 people had made their own bélo. In a very literal way, the brand is shared and made by its users, not its original owner.

Already there's a backlash against the 'platform' idea. Businesses like Uber are heavily criticized for taking work away from traditional, regulated taxi drivers. In Germany, for example, the new highly individualized 'Plattform-Kapitalismus' is seen as threatening more traditional, more organized ways of working, where there was solidarity among, rather than competition between, workers.

So branding is still about persuasion, where the producer asserts power, but it is also increasingly about making a useful platform, where the consumer exerts power, and indeed becomes a producer. In this context, the role of the brand, at least for the moment, is to bring more and more users onto the platform, and to keep them there: to produce network effects. This is, as we saw in Chapter 3, branding version 5.

Where will this power struggle go next? One view is that technology will give the consumer more power than the producer. Given enough data, and effective comparison websites, consumers will have complete information about the marketplace, and will base all their buying decisions on a perfect knowledge of all the facts. On this view, brands become much less important. In their book *Absolute Value*, Itamar Simonson and Emanuel Rosen give a clear example: 'You always knew what to expect at Subway or McDonald's. But when you know what to expect at a small restaurant through Yelp or Zagat, brand names are becoming relatively less important.' Of course, you could take the opposite view: as comparison sites force up standards and therefore encourage homogeneity, the non-rational things, the features beyond the facts, will become more important in helping me chose what's right for me.

Another version of the future posits a switch from 'customer relationship management'—the databases the big companies keep about us—to 'vendor relationship management'. In this new world, set out by Doc Searls in *The Intention Economy*, the tables are turned: consumers now keep tabs on producers, we all have databases about them. Instead of companies launching campaigns to sell their products to us, we'll launch campaigns to announce our needs and goals (our 'intentions') to the world, and companies will bid to meet them. If I need a new fridge, I'll declare this intention online, and Bosch, Beko, Candy, Haier, and the rest will fight among themselves to make me the best offer. Again, this could make branding irrelevant. Or it could mean that the brand is part of what the company offers us—the meaning as well as the functionality. Or it could even mean that our own individual personal brands will help us attract the very best deals from the companies.

How should branding feel?

Alongside the changing shape of the corporation, and the shifting power of the consumer, a third storyline is discernible, to do with the culture of branding: the way that brand managers and brand consultants feel about what they do.

The traditional way of thinking favours single-mindedness. Ever since the advertising guru David Ogilvy started talking about the 'big idea', marketing people—and their advisors—have been unifiers, simplifiers, and rationalizers. The discipline of corporate identity design, now usually called brand consulting, was founded on an impulse to take a mess of different brand names, logos, and messages and turn it into a beautifully organized organization. This transformation would be shaped by an overarching thought. Wally Olins, one of the most influential proponents of this approach, talked about the importance of the 'central idea': one single concept from which every piece of communication and design would flow. The core concept is *identity*. An organization needs to have a single identity, consistent across time and space, in order to flourish, and the logo is the marker of that identity.

This way of thinking meshes well with the traditional approaches of business schools and management consultancies, where organizations are imagined as highly disciplined entities, governed by an overarching strategy. This is the approach of the architect or master-planner: businesses in general, and brands in particular, are best constructed from a blueprint.

The mainstream of organizational thinking is that, in the words of Thomas Friedman, 'the world is flat'. In this view, the victory of capitalism, and the incredibly rapid spread of smartphones and social media, mean that the world is pretty much the same everywhere. A big idea can work universally, and the goal of every start-up is to 'scale' their business, so that the same software that served a hundred customers can serve a billion.

Most big global brands use something like the big idea approach. BMW, for instance, is still the 'ultimate driving machine', a slogan first used in 1975. Microsoft is still very much the same everywhere in the world. And newer brands from India and China tend to emulate this kind of thinking, where a brand is built through a consistent logo, slogan, colours, and communication style. Indeed, recent research suggests that these traditional branding tools are still extremely effective at burning brands into people's minds.

Against the formula

But the last ten years or so have seen the rise of a contrary view: that plurality, complication, and even messiness might be a good thing. The thinking is that the world moves too fast for blueprints. Five-year strategies and ten-year brand positionings are out-of-date as soon as they're written. In addition, customers don't want imposed ideas. They will shape what a brand is about much more effectively than the brand's owner can control it. And, it's argued, the world *isn't* flat: cultures still differ enormously, and management by formula never quite works. Indeed, the secret to attracting the commitment of customers may be to create variety, localness, and constant novelty.

Finally, many practitioners now feel differently about branding. A mistrust has developed for the formula, a boredom with the sameness of brands, a fatigue with the big idea. Instead of focusing on a single brand *identity*, practitioners talk about designing a multifaceted customer *experience*.

This is the approach not of the architect but what academics call the *bricoleur*—the handyperson, the do-it-yourself-er—making things out of whatever lies to hand, and learning by trial and error.

The explosion of technology start-ups has encouraged this new mood. In these businesses, neat, single-minded strategies and business plans are rejected in favour of rapid, multiple experiments. Success comes not from intellectual neatness but creative messiness. Methods used in software engineering—agility, rapid prototyping, sprints, independent teams—have been transplanted into management philosophy, and the summit of this conceptual mountain is a radically decentralized management approach called 'holacracy', meaning a hierarchy of units that are simultaneously autonomous and interdependent.

In branding, the most obvious symptom is visual—the emergence of variant, generative, and animated logos. In 2000, Tate launched four different versions of its logo, and a decade later, MIT Media Lab announced a new logo with 40,000 self-generating variants—though both have subsequently been simplified. Google frequently runs a special logo-of-the-day, called a Doodle. AOL's logo is white on white, invisible until something else moves behind it: it was designed to be not static but animated.

Brand as pattern

Branding experts talk about 'liquid brands' or 'moving brands', but they mean more than just liquid logos or moving logos. They mean that the ideas behind the logo are themselves much less fixed. Experience design expert Marc Shillum has argued that branding is about 'creating patterns, not repeating messages'. It's an interplay of many small ideas, not one big idea. Starbucks has moved away from a formulaic approach to its coffee shops, preferring, it says, 'identity to identical'.

Branding from beyond the West may be pointing the way. Mandarin Oriental, from Hong Kong, is a hotel group that has broken out of the Western, formulaic model. Muji has built a retail brand by rejecting the more ostentatious modes of Western branding. China's innovative 'content ecosystem' business LeEco is building a brand that spans Eastern and Western styles. Huawei is not a conventional corporation, and may well therefore develop a different kind of brand. Distinctively African brands are now playing on the world stage, like Jumia or the South African shoe maker Sole Rebels.

The drama here is that many organizations flip from control to liberation and back again. Coca-Cola is master of the formula, and yet also embraces liberation, printing multiple labels with not one brand name but a wide range of first names—Erin, Kelly, Rebecca, Tim, and so on, in the Coca-Cola typeface. Yet this, of course, is just a more sophisticated kind of formula. The big internet brands are loose and multiple in some ways, and yet still depend on a consistent name, logo, and user interface to create network effects. And most of the new Eastern brands—though oriental in management style—emulate the branding techniques of the West: in the airline industry, Emirates and IndiGo are two very successful examples. We're seeing a constantly shifting interplay between traditional consistency, based on a tight sense of brand identity, and a looser kind of coherence, based on a more plural sense of brand experience.

Death and life

All three of these storylines question the future of branding. If organizations become looser organisms, will they need or want brands? If customers become more powerful than producers, will brands become irrelevant? If the trend from consistency to pattern grows, will branding, as we know it, gradually disappear?

My view is that branding will continue to be essential, but that it will become less formal, less pompous, less monolithic, less institutional, less purely commercial, less corporate. In scope, branding will reach less formal kinds of organization, and even the biggest will try to look smaller and more informal. Indeed, we're just at the beginning of a shift to the start-up and the social enterprise and the idea of 'open-source' technologies. In role, branding will aim not to persuade people just to buy, but enlist people to take part. And in style, branding will less and less follow the Western model: it will be less tight and controlled and neat and consistent in its form. We're just at the beginning of the rise of Asian and African brands.

Of course, these three storylines are closely interrelated: looser, less controlled organizations suit the needs of powerful, active consumers, and are best expressed through looser, less consistent branding. This dynamic is set to accelerate.

Branding, in other words, will live on. The human practice of creating value by using marks on objects to make meanings will always be with us.

References

Chapter 1: The triumph of branding

Coca-Cola in Africa

<http://www.coca-colacompany.com/stories/
coca-cola-offers-consumers-reasons-to-believe>

80% of marketing directors believe their products are differentiated

<https://hbr.org/2012/03/living-differentiation>

People wouldn't care if 74% of brands disappeared

<http://www.havasmedia.com/press/press-releases/2015/
top-scoring-meaningful-brands-enjoy-a-share-of-wallet-46-
per-cent-higher-than-low-performers>

Brand accounts for more than 30% of the stockmarket value

<http://www.economist.com/news/business/21614150-brands-
are-most-valuable-assets-many-companies-possess-no-one-
agrees-how-much-they>

Chapter 2: What is 'branding'?

Definitions of 'brand'

Kornberger, Martin (2010). *Brand Society*. Cambridge: Cambridge
University Press.

Barden, Phil (2013). *Decoded*. Chichester: John Wiley.

Aaker, David A. and Joachimsthaler, Erich (2009). *Brand Leadership*.
London: Simon & Schuster.

Keller, Kevin Lane (2012). *Strategic Brand Management*. London: Pearson.

Neumeier, Marty (2006). *The Brand Gap*. Berkeley, CA: New Riders.

Chapter 3: The history of branding

The Cadbury story

Cadbury, Deborah (2010). *Chocolate Wars*. London: HarperPress.

A 1955 article

Gardner, B. B. and Levy, Sidney J. (1955). The Product and the Brand. *Harvard Business Review* 33/2 (March–April): 33–9.

The producer-consumer

Toffler, Alvin (1980). *The Third Wave*. New York: Willam Morrow.

No visible logo

<http://www.independent.co.uk/life-style/fashion/news/how-anonymous-designers-are-trading-on-their-creators-lack-of-ego-10433788.html>

Chapter 4: How branding works

System 1 thinking

Kahneman, Daniel (2011). *Thinking, Fast and Slow*. New York: Farrar, Straus and Giroux.

A brand is an upstream reservoir

<http://www.britishbrandsgroup.org.uk/upload/File/Lecture-1.pdf>

Loving the brand

Batra, Rajeev, Ahuvia, Aaron, and Bagozzi, Richard P. (2012). Brand Love. *Journal of Marketing* 76: 1–16.

A study by management consultants

<http://www.forbes.com/sites/marketshare/2012/03/26/only-one-quarter-of-american-consumers-are-brand-loyal/#13afab486e9a>

Loyal switchers

Sharp, Byron (2010). *How Brands Grow*. Oxford: Oxford University Press.

Brand equity

Keller, Kevin Lane (2012). *Strategic Brand Management*. London:
    Pearson.

BrandZ's valuation of the Google brand

<http://www.millwardbrown.com/brandz/top-global-brands/2016>

Chapter 5: The branding business

Deep inside Procter & Gamble

<http://www.brandingstrategyinsider.com/2009/06/great-moments-
    in-branding-neil-mcelroy-memo.html>

Strategic brand leadership

Aaker, David A. and Joachimsthaler, Erich (2009). *Brand Leadership*.
    London: Simon & Schuster.

A 2015 survey

<http://marketing.hallandpartners.com/acton/attachment/6945/
    f-0598/1/-/-/-/-/2015%2007%2009%20-%20IPA%20Booklet.pdf>

Chapter 6: Branding projects

The Ryanair story

Interview with Kenny Jacobs, 2015.

Jeff Bezos on 70% shouting

<http://www.forbes.com/global/2012/0507/global-2000-12-amazon-
    jeff-bezos-gets-it.html>

Tony Hseih on 'your culture is your brand'

<http://www.huffingtonpost.com/tony-hsieh/zappos-founder-tony-
    hsieh_1_b_783333.html>

Chapter 7: The ethics of branding

Three critics

Packard, Vance (1957). *The Hidden Persuaders*. New York: David
    McKay.
Berger, John (1972). *Ways of Seeing*. London: BBC.
Klein, Naomi (1999). *No Logo*. Toronto: Knopf.

Chapter 8: A future for branding?

Active consumers

<http://www.bbc.co.uk/blogs/bbcinternet/2012/05/bbc_online_
briefing_spring_201_1.html>

Your brand is what they say it is

Neumeier, Marty (2015). *The Brand Flip*. Berkeley, CA: New Riders.

The mainstream of organizational thinking

Friedman, Thomas (2005). *The World is Flat*. New York: Farrar,
Straus and Giroux.

Further reading

I hope this book has opened your eyes to some of the ways branding works in today's world. If so, you may want to look more deeply into the subject. There are thousands of books and other resources: this is my short-list of the most rewarding ones.

The two academic giants of branding are Kevin Lane Keller and David Aaker. If you like big and encyclopedic textbooks, then Keller's *Strategic Brand Management* (Pearson, 2012) is exhaustive and up-to-date; and it's also worth reading Aaker's *Building Strong Brands* (Simon & Schuster, 2002).

The other most widely read textbooks are *Creating Powerful Brands* by Leslie de Chernatony, Malcolm McDonald, and Elaine Wallace (Routledge, 2011) and Jean-Noël Kapferer's *The New Strategic Brand Management* (Kogan Page, 2012).

For an overview of academic theories about branding, *Brand Management* by Tilde Heding, Charlotte F. Knudtzen, and Mogens Bjerre (Routledge, 2016) is beautifully organized and invaluable.

If, like me, you're fascinated by the central role brands play in our lives as consumers and workers, then read Martin Kornberger's *Brand Society* (Cambridge University Press, 2010): a masterly overview of how brand drives both production (how it influences management) and consumption (how it influences lifestyles). You may also enjoy Adam Arvidsson's challenging book *Brands: Meaning and Value in Media Culture* (Routledge, 2006).

To drill into the role branding can play in management, look at the fascinating *Taking Brand Initiative* by Mary Jo Hatch and Majken Schultz (Jossey Bass, 2008). It's also worth reading David Aaker and Erich Joachimsthaler's book *Brand Leadership* (Simon & Schuster, 2009), which makes a strong case for treating brand as a central and strategic and long-term organizational asset. For a sceptical counterpoint, try *Simply Better* by Patrick Barwise and Seán Mehan (Harvard Business School Press, 2004), and, even more thought-provoking, John Kay's book *Obliquity* (Profile, 2010).

For an overview of the subject from the point of view of practitioners, I recommend the work of two writers, Marty Neumeier and Wally Olins. Neumeier's latest book, *The Brand Flip* (New Riders, 2015), is energetic and brilliantly designed. And Wally Olins's final book, *Brand New* (Thames & Hudson, 2014) is a worthy summation of an extraordinarily influential career. You'll also enjoy Debbie Millman's interviews with a range of practitioners in *Brand Thinking* (Allworth Press, 2011).

To find out more about how brands actually work, read Byron Sharp's *How Brands Grow* (Oxford University Press, 2010), a wonderfully nonconformist analysis, questioning (rightly, in my view) ideas like brand loyalty, positioning, and differentiation. And *Decoded* by Phil Barden (Wiley, 2013) is a refreshingly clear account of what behavioural economics and neuroscience tell us about how brands make us buy things.

Finally, to explore design in branding, look at Alina Wheeler's *Designing Brand Identity* (Wiley, 2013), which is comprehensive and (as you'd hope) fully illustrated; and Michael Johnson's energetically visual exploration, *Branding in Five and a Half Steps* (Thames & Hudson, 2016).

Index

SOCIAL MEDIA
Very Short Introduction

Join our community

www.oup.com/vsi

- Join us online at the official Very Short Introductions **Facebook** page.
- Access the thoughts and musings of our authors with our online **blog**.
- Sign up for our monthly **e-newsletter** to receive information on all new titles publishing that month.
- Browse the full range of Very Short Introductions online.
- Read **extracts** from the Introductions for free.
- If you are a teacher or lecturer you can order inspection copies quickly and simply via our website.

GLOBALIZATION
A Very Short Introduction
Manfred Steger

'Globalization' has become one of the defining buzzwords of our time - a term that describes a variety of accelerating economic, political, cultural, ideological, and environmental processes that are rapidly altering our experience of the world. It is by its nature a dynamic topic - and this *Very Short Introduction* has been fully updated for 2009, to include developments in global politics, the impact of terrorism, and environmental issues. Presenting globalization in accessible language as a multifaceted process encompassing global, regional, and local aspects of social life, Manfred B. Steger looks at its causes and effects, examines whether it is a new phenomenon, and explores the question of whether, ultimately, globalization is a good or a bad thing.

www.oup.com/vsi